Food Intake and Nutritional Status of Rural Household

Food Intake and Nutritional Status of Rural Household

Dr. Kolli Ravi Kumar
Ph.D.

SERIALS PUBLICATIONS
NEW DELHI (INDIA)

First Published - 2010

ISBN: 978-81-8387-414-4

Published by

SERIALS PUBLICATIONS
4830/24, 1st Floor, Ansari Road
Darya Ganj, New Delhi-110002 (India)
Phone : 23245225. Fax : 91-11-23272135
E-mail : serials@sify.com
serialspublications.india@gmail.com
Website : www.serialspublications.com

DEDICATION TO THE LOVING MEMORY OF

Late Dr. Y.S. Rajasekhar Reddy Garu

Former Chief Minister of Andhra Pradesh, a modern Sir Arthur Cotton of India, who made an unprecedented and unparalleled attempt to wipe out undernourishment of the rural folks through an innovative concept of "JALAYAGNAM" in the state.

CONTENTS

PREFACE

India since independence made great strides on several fronts (technological break-troughs, industrial and agricultural revolutions, IT and ITES) which pushed its growth trajectory into the range of 8-9 percent, as a result of which it emerged from the backwaters of underdevelopment during mid-20th century to the centre stage of world economic powers. Sever food shortages of '50s and '60s were wiped out by successful green revolution in irrigated tracts of the country leading to surplus of wheat and rice stocks and their export by '90s. But yet, incidence of malnutrition among its people more particularly among rural population has been more or less the same around 50 percent over the last half a century. The National Sample Survey Organization (NSSO), the National Institute of Nutrition (NIN) and the National Family Health Survey (NFHS) have been conducting periodic nation–wide repeat surveys on food intake and nutritional status of Indian people. Though the type of data and the methods of their collection vary from organization to organization, their findings are the same-nearly half of the population is under-nourished and its prevalence is more among vulnerable people(children, women and old people) than among adult males.

The NSSO collects household monthly food expenditure data by recall method, the NIN collects data on food intake by the individual family members in the last 24 hours prior to the date of the survey along with data on the four ınthropometric parameters, while the NFHS collects data on the frequency of intake of selected health foods, height, weight and age of women and children.

As against this background, Dr. Ravikumar's study on food intake and nutritional status of rural households in coastal Andhra is a bit different. It appears that he believed that irrigation is a strongly influencing factor in food consumption as it affects both family income and availability of perishable health food items such as fruits, vegetables, fish and milk in rural areas. He made a comparative study of food intake and nutritional status of different caste and occupational groups in a rain-fed agriculture dependent village in Vizayanagaram district and a fully canal irrigated village in East Godavari district of Coastal Andhra. His methodology of study is some what different from others. In addition to the usual study of food intake and nutritional status, he collected some interesting data on time and frequency food preparation in the household, intra-family differences in the consumption frequency of household prepared food items at each meal. Such data collected by recall method is highly unreliable compare to quantities of food intake as no body makes a weighment of them at any time. On the other hand, recollection of prepared food items consumed is very easy and highly reliable. Dr. Ravikumar must be commended for breaking from the routine and for taking up a new approach. I hope readers will find it quite interesting. I wish the author will continue his studies on the same topic in future also.

I wish him great success in life.

Prof. Prasad Reddy, P.V.G.D
Registrar, Andhra University

ACKNOWLEDGEMENTS

The present study is based on my *Ph.D.* thesis submitted to and approved by Andhra University for the award of the Degree of Doctor of Philosophy in *2007*. At the outset. I will be failing in my duty if I do not acknowledge the help, received from Prof. *Beela Satyanarayana,* the Hon'ble Vice Chancellor and *Prof. P.V.G.D. Prasad Reddy,* Registrar, Andhra University respectively in bringing out my thesis for publication. I acknowledge with thanks the three adjudicators for their comments and suggestions which improved the quality of the work.

I wish to acknowledge my debt and gratitude to my Research Director, *Prof. Kata Venkata Reddy,* and Joint Director, *Prof. D.PullaRao,* Department of Co-operation and Applied Economics for their valuable guidance at every stage of the work.

I am beholden to *Prof. L.K. Mohan Rao,* Principal, Andhra University College of Arts and Commerce, and Honorary Director, *Agro Economic Research Centre* for the kind co-operation and encouragement provided in every stage of my work. I sincerely thank Prof. S. Ramesh Babu, Chairman, Board of Studies and Prof. R. Rama Krishna, Head of the Department for their encouragement at every stage of the work. I extend my sincere thanks to Prof. E. Nagabhushana Rao and Prof. N. Bhaskara Reddy for their good wishes for completing the thesis work.

I am deeply indebted to *Prof. D.S. Prasad* for editing the final draft and *Dr. Bhamidipati Padmanarayana* for her help in computer analysis of the data.

I am also thankful to M. Venkata Rao typist and other office staff of the department for the kind cooperation extended in the completion of my work.

I would like to express my sincere gratitude to Mr.K.Raghuvaraprasad librarian, School of Economics and the staff members of the Dr.V.S. Krishna Memorial Library, Andhra University for providing me with all the necessary material. I am very much grateful to all my co-research scholars, D. Ashalatha, Jayasheela Prakash, S. Appala Naidu, P. Appa Rao, Gorli Srinivas, Gorja Venugopal, Datti Sanka Rao and Datti Sriram for their cooperation in collecting the data.

I would also like to express my gratefulness to my father. K. Simha Chalam, mother Sureedu, uncles V. Appala Swamy, V. Sreeram, aunties V. Savitri, and V. Sasikala and my brother Tirupati Venkata Ramana his wife Bharati, and my nephews V. Krishna, V. Bharatiraja, his wife Jyothikumari, V. Purdhviraj, V. Praneeth Kumar and V. Sivunnaidu, niece Bhavanibaburao, other family members, friends and relatives who encouraged me to join the Doctoral programm and supported me morally and financially all through my work. A good number of generous individuals have inspired me and extended their cooperation at various stages of my research work directly or indirectly. I owe a lot to each one of them.

Finally, I would like to thank SERIALS PUBLICATIONS, New Delhi for their kind efforts in neat and speedy publication of the work.

KOLLI RAVI KUMAR

1

INTRODUCTION

INTRODUCTION

Generally it is argued that low agricultural production and lack of an appropriate food distribution system are the reasons for low levels of the nutritional status. In addition to low agricultural production, the low nutritional status of the rural population is to be viewed as the problem of poor quality of food intake due to low literacy and lack of awareness.

Food Consumption in Various Countries

Economic development is normally accompanied by improvements in a country's food supply and gradual elimination of dietary deficiencies, thus improving the overall nutritional status of the country's population. Furthermore, the development also brings about qualitative changes in the production, processing, distribution and marketing of food. Increasing urbanization will also have consequences for the dietary patterns and lifestyles of individuals, not all of which are positive. Moreover, the pace of these changes seems to be accelerating, especially in the low-income and middle-income countries. At the same time, however, poor countries continue to face food shortages and nutrient inadequacies. Presently, in India one percent or 10 million people are not getting two square meals a day[1]. Food consumption expressed in kilocalories (k.cal) per capita per day is a key variable used for measuring and evaluating the evolution of the global and regional food situation. A more appropriate term for this variable would be "national average apparent food consumption" since the data come from National Food Balance Sheets rather than from food consumption surveys. Analysis of FAOSTAT data shows that dietary energy measured in k.cals per capita per day has been steadily increasing on a worldwide basis; availability of calories per capita from the mid-1960s to the late 1990s increased globally by approximately 450 k.cal per capita per day and by over 600 k.cal per capita per day in developing countries (Table 1). This change has not, however, been equal across regions. The per capita supply of calories has remained almost stagnant in sub-Saharan Africa and has recently fallen in the countries in economic transition. In contrast, the per capita supply of energy has risen dramatically in East Asia (by almost 1000 k.cal per capita per day, mainly in China) and in the Near East/North Africa region (by over 700 k.cal per capita per day)[2]. The agriculture seasons and irrigation facilities will influence the food intake of the households. For example, in Combodia between harvests to lean season most rural households face 5 to 30 percent reduction in their rice intake. Even in Tailand there is a difference in food intake in the wet season and dry season, especially among the mountainous regions.[3]

Table 1
Global and Regional Per Capita Food Consumption
(K.Cal per capita per day)

Region	*1964–1966*	*1974–1976*	*1984–1986*	*1997–1999*	*2015*	*2030*
World	2358	2435	2655	2803	2940	3050
Developing countries	2054	2152	2450	2681	2850	2980
Near East and North Africa	2290	2591	2953	3006	3090	3170
Sub-Saharan Africa[a]	2058	2079	2057	2195	2360	2540
Latin America and the Caribbean	2393	2546	2689	2824	2980	3140
East Asia	1957	2105	2559	2921	3060	3190
South Asia	2017	1986	2205	2403	2700	2900
Industrialized countries	2947	3065	3206	3380	3440	3500
Transition countries	3222	3385	3379	2906	3060	3180

Source: *Literature, Food Consumption and Nutrition Division, International Food Policy Research Institute, Discussion Paper No. 19.*

Not only that the differences in food intake also exist within household due to some preferences and these are more prominent based on the seasonal variations. In South Asia, with considerable variation within that region, the evidence on food distribution within the household suggests that, while there is some pro-male and pro-adult bias in terms of the quantity of food intake. Inequality may also be affected by seasonality, with lower inequality during the harvest as opposed to the lean season[4].

Food and Nutrition

Food provides energy, helps in repairing damaged parts of cells and tissues and also makes new material necessary for growth and reproduction of living beings. The major components of food are: carbohydrates, proteins, fats, vitamins and minerals. These are called nutrients. It is needless to emphasize the importance of data on intake levels of nutrients of the persons of a country for understanding their general health status. The measures of nutritional intake status also indicate the availability of adequate food to the people.

Foodgrain production had nearly kept place with population growth. However, while average per capita foodgrain availability nearly corresponds to pre capita requirements, in view of gross iniquities with regard to food distribution, large proportion of poor households do not have access to adequate food. India's nutrition problem is thus not so much one of lack of adequate access to food. In over 30 percent of poor households whose family incomes are so low even if 70 per cent of family income is spent on food, nutritional needs are not met[5]

New challenges and opportunities for augmenting food production are now unfolding with recent advances in biotechnology and genetic engineering given our rich biodiversity and our large scientific manpower we are richly endowed with the capabilities to respond to the new challenges. Research, designed to identify high nutritive value varieties of fruits and vegetables and genetic engineering to maximize yields and nutritive value of a wide range of food, will need to be supported[6].

Inspite of early apprehensions, foodgrain production in India has kept pace with population, acute large-scale famines, which used to occur periodically before independence had now been eliminated. Inspite of this, a large proportion of poor households across India does not have access to adequate food due to lack of purchasing power. About 35 per cent or around 325 million Indians spend over 70 per cent of the family income to meet food and nutritional needs. The quinquennial consumer expenditure surveys of the NSSO make the estimation of the per capita consumption of different food items and consequent supply of energy, proteins, fat. These estimates are presented at the all India level according to expenditure class categories. According to this analysis food and nutrition deficiencies are much larger than poverty estimates[7].

Sustainable Food Production to meet Nutritional Needs

Nutritionists view agricultural as input for dietary intake while farmers look for returns for their investment. The green revolution showed that food grain production could be increased four fold if farmers are assured of returns for their investment (Figure 1). However, pulse and coarse grain production has stagnated[8].

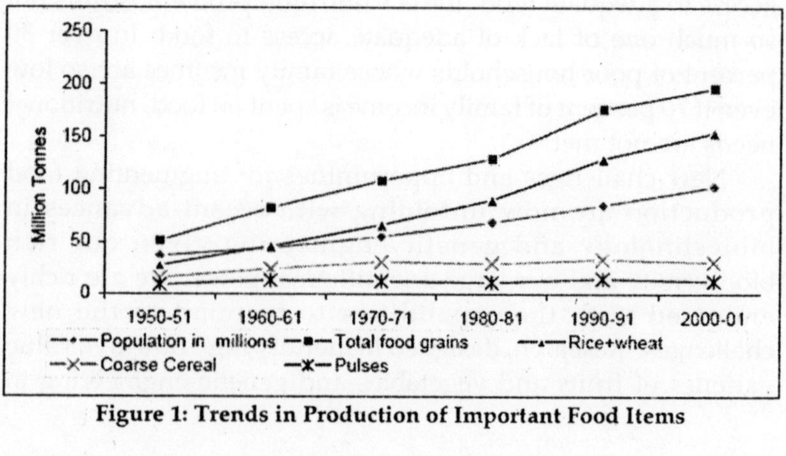

Figure 1: Trends in Production of Important Food Items

Over the last five decades, per capita net availability of cereals has been showing improvement and by 1991 it was sufficient to meet the Recommended Dietary Allowances (RDA) (Figure 2). However, the per capita pulse availability and consumption, has declined. Pulses are major source of protein among the poorer segments of the population and so this trend has to be reversed[9].

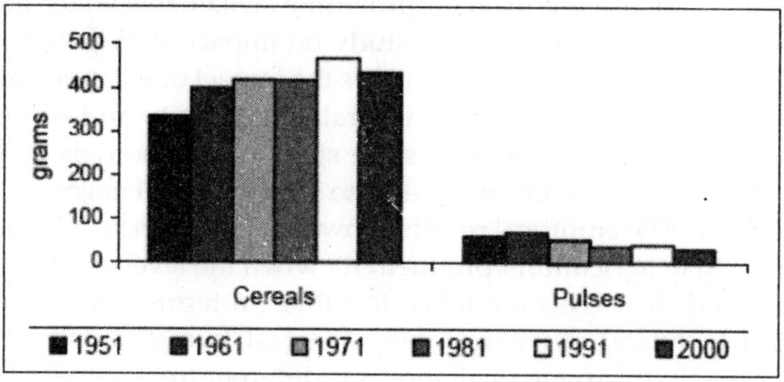

Figure 2: Per capita Net Availability/day

The agro-nutritional classification of foods and its expression in the form of a nutritional dose reveals three major peculiarities in the Indian agro nutritional profile. The average calorie intake is fairly low, 2,415 K.cal per capita per day[10], as against 2,619 for all developing countries 2,745 at the world level and 3,177 for developed countries in 1996. A world agro nutritional classification based on FAO's averages for the three year period extending from 1975 to 1977 placed India under the type traditionally agricultural based on cereals where cereals and starchy roots contribute more than 70 percent of the total dietary energy supply.

Irrigation and Agricultural Productivity

Water, as an input to agriculture, is critical for sustaining the food security. India faces the daunting task of increasing its food grain production by over 50 per cent in the next two decades. Increasing competition for water in agriculture, industry, domestic and environment uses is already manifested in inter- and intra-sector, basin, state, district and village level conflicts. India Water Vision, 2025 estimated the gross water demand for multiple uses to double in 25 years from now with corresponding investment needs of Rs 20,000 crore per year[12]. To achieve the targeted annual agricultural growth rate of over 4% in the Tenth Five Year Plan, irrigation sector should grow by at least 5% per annum, given 1% growth in rainfed sector. Demand-supply management in water sector and efficiency in its every use is critical for providing sustainable water-food security to the country. The study on impact of irrigation on agriculture and poverty quantifies the impact of irrigation and other factor inputs on agricultural productivity and on two key poverty measures across the states[13]. The Study is based on the time series data from 1970 to 1994 for the 14 major states of India. The empirical results show that there is no significant growth in agricultural productivity when the level of all input use and their costs are taken together (in terms of economic and technical efficiency) over the last two decades. This productivity growth of all inputs is different from simple crop yield or labour productivity. The changing trends in irrigation and land and labor productivity are shown in Figure 3. The regression results of the Study show that the marginal impact of irrigation on growth of productivity of all inputs is positive

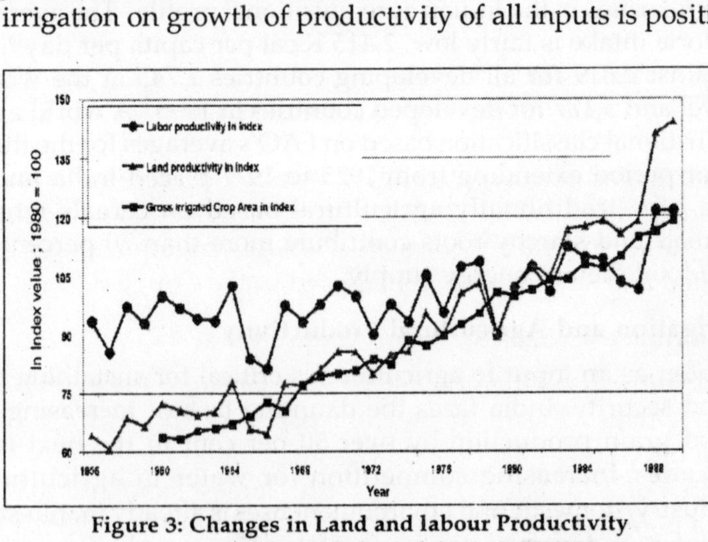

Figure 3: Changes in Land and labour Productivity and Gross Irrigated Area, 1956-1989

and significant with an elasticity of 0.32. This means that one percent increase in irrigated area has brought about an increase of about 0.32 percent in the productivity of all inputs (TFP) in India during 1970-94.

Despite annual expansion in the created potential and capital investments in irrigation sector, the area irrigated by the major, medium and minor irrigation systems has been either stagnating or declining from mid-1980s and during 1990s, as witnessed in some major states (Fig. 4).

For instance, currently in Uttar Pradesh canals are irrigating 30.6 lakh ha in 2000 as against 33.3 lakh ha in 1985 Similarly, in Andhra Pradesh, canals now irrigate 11% less area than what

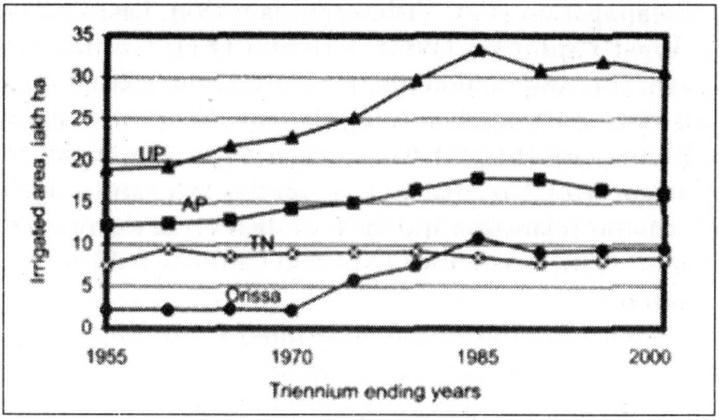

Figure 4: Performance of Canal Irrigation System

was irrigated 15 years ago. Bihar, Orissa and Tamil Nadu also recorded a similar decline in the canal irrigated area[14]. These five states together account for 50% of irrigation potential created and 45% of net area irrigated in the Country.

Importance of Agriculture in Andhra Pradesh

Agriculture is the mainstay of the economy in Andhra Pradesh (AP) with its wide diversified farm base; is a foodgrain surplus state-often called the granary of south. Andhra Pradesh, with an area of 2,75,000 sq kms is the fifth largest state in India. It has a population of 2001 census, with a large majority (73.2%)

living in rural areas in 29,400 villages and the balance (26.8%) living in about 250 urban towns and cities. Nearly 20.8% of the population is Scheduled Castes (14.9%) and Scheduled Tribes (5.9%). According to the 2001 census, overall literacy rate in the state is 37.4% as compared with an average of 52.1% in the country. Female literacy, as in many other states in the country is lower (28.0%) than male literacy (46.6%). These figures are again much lower than the all-India figures of 39.4% and 63.9% respectively.

The state is divided into 23 districts spread over three distinct geographical regions known as Coastal Andhra, Rayalaseema and Telangana. The nine districts of Srikakulam (Sr), Vizianagaram (Vz), Vishakapatnam (Vs), East Godavari (EG), West Godavari (WG), Krishna (Kr), Guntur (Gu), Prakasam (Pr) and Nellore (Ne) constitute the coastal region. Ten districts of Hyderabad (Hy), Rangareddy (Ra), Nalgonda (Na), Khammam (Kh), Mahboobnagar (Ma), Warangal (Wa), Karimnagar (Ka), Nizamabad (Ni), Medak (Me) and Adilabad (Ad) form the Telangana and the four districts of Kurnool (Ku), Cuddapah (Cu), Anantapur (An) and Chittoor (Ch) make up Rayalaseema.

The concentration of the Scheduled Caste population is highest (20.7%) in Nellore district and lowest (7%) in Vishakapatnam. The tribal population is most concentrated (24.5%) in Khammam district and least in Hyderabad (0.64%).

Andhra Pradesh is blessed with many major rivers, the most important being Godavari, Krishna, Vamsadhara and Pennar. The State's share of dependable flows from these river systems is estimated to be 2,746 thousand million cubic feet (TMC). This breaks up into 1,495 TMC from Godavari river system, 811 TMC from Krishna, 98 TMC from the Pennar and the rest from other smaller rivers.

About 40% of the gross cropped area in the State is irrigated, and its contribution to State agricultural production is about 60%. It is in irrigated areas where the bulk of agricultural growth has occurred. Irrigation has also resulted in alleviation of poverty in upland and backward areas, by

Figure 5: Map of Andhra Pradesh

providing sustained income to farmers, increasing in wage employment and availability of water for human and cattle consumption and industrial activities[15]. Most development strategies for agriculture focused predominantly in irrigated areas. These areas have benefited immensely from the 'Green Revolution', used modern technology, had high productivity and generally prosperous. However, to realise the goals of equitable development and growth of 6 per cent per annum for the next 25 years, the focus needs to shift to developing the backward, drought-prone and rain-fed areas (also referred to as dryland areas) which form roughly 60 per cent of the total gross cropped area. These areas get their water only from rainfall or ground water and, therefore, do not have assured irrigation[16].

Andhra Pradesh receives rains from the South-West (SW) as well as North-East (North East) monsoons. The monsoon is the South-West monsoon contributes nearly two thirds of rainfall (600 mm), while the NE monsoon (Oct-Dec), supplies the remaining one-third. On average, the coastal region receives the highest rainfall (1000 mm) followed by Telengana (890 mm) and Rayalaseema (670 mm). Periodic droughts in Telengana and Rayalaseema regions and floods in Coastal Andhra however, hamper food production in the State.

Agriculture is the major strength of the AP economy and it provides livelihood to 70% of its population. It is estimated that 36.2% of the state's net domestic product is derived from agriculture. Major crops grown in the State are: rice, *jowar, bajra, ragi* (millets), maize, sugar cane, chillies, groundnut, castor, cotton, and tobacco. Rice is the principal food crop followed by *jowar* and other coarse millets. Among the cash crops, sugar cane, cotton and tobacco are important. The major oil seed produced in the State is ground nut. A variety of pulses are also produced. The State recorded an improvement in food production in the late 1970s and early 1980s through adoption of improved management techniques, despite an almost constant area under food grains. About 68% of arable lands in the State are reported to be under dry farming and cultivated by poor farmers. Special efforts are being made to increase production of food grains, oil seeds and commercial crops through active programmes in watershed development, soil and moisture conservation, crop insurance, cattle breeding, horticulture and floriculture.

Food and Nutrition Security

Food security has been a major goal of development policy in India since the beginning of planning. Food availability and price stability were considered measures of food security till

Table 2
Agricultural Production in Andhra Pradesh during 1956- 2006

(ml.tones/year)

Years	Rice	Jowar	Bajra	Maize	Ragi	Total cereals	Green gram	Black gram	Red gram	Bengal gram	Horse gram	Total Pulses	Total food grains	Ground nut	Castor	Sesa-mum	Cotton	Tobacco	Sugar cane	Chillies
1956-57	34.07	11.08	2.99	1.05	2.91	56.16	0.67	0.29	0.43	0.33	0.9	2.76	58.92	12.22	0.65	0.53	1.33	1.35	6.29	1.15
1957-58	33.46	12.74	3.26	1.2	2.36	56.91	0.61	0.33	0.43	0.33	0.77	2.59	59.5	10.7	0.32	0.47	1.35	1.15	6.47	0.82
1958-59	37.64	14.66	3.47	1.61	2.94	64.91	0.61	0.35	0.42	0.31	0.8	2.61	67.52	9.13	0.44	0.45	1.22	1.35	6.79	0.76
1959-60	38.36	14.77	3.16	1	3.38	64.92	0.78	0.36	0.38	0.27	0.83	2.73	67.65	7.54	0.53	0.37	1.01	1.12	6.8	0.8
1960-61	36.61	13.56	2.97	1.55	2.9	61.45	0.68	0.33	0.63	0.24	0.76	2.76	64.21	6.94	0.57	0.34	1.2	1.13	8.13	0.84
1961-62	45.15	14.48	3.7	2.15	3.4	72.97	0.73	0.39	0.72	0.27	0.84	3.1	76.07	5.28	0.54	0.45	1.31	1.27	7.9	0.84
1962-63	42.43	14.05	3.51	1.63	2.9	68.71	0.78	0.4	0.44	0.27	0.9	2.96	71.67	6.64	0.47	0.54	1.22	1.32	8.2	0.89
1963-64	43.43	13.94	3.33	1.63	2.93	69.41	0.79	0.43	0.56	0.26	0.91	3.11	72.52	7.54	0.47	0.42	1.4	1.76	10.78	1.3
1964-65	50.07	11.38	2.87	2.57	2.92	73.63	0.8	0.53	0.87	0.24	0.83	3.41	77.04	9.14	0.54	0.42	1.53	1.55	12.18	1.28
1965-66	39.61	10.16	2.41	1.83	2.34	58.28	0.61	0.41	0.67	0.18	0.73	2.7	60.98	6.3	0.38	0.39	0.83	1.28	10.94	0.84
1966-67	44.15	12.06	3.7	1.73	2.63	66.77	0.65	0.35	0.74	0.17	0.54	2.56	69.33	8.19	0.63	0.54	1.45	1.72	8.43	1.08
1967-68	46.74	11.98	2.91	2.57	2.77	69.15	0.69	0.39	0.85	0.2	0.55	2.78	71.93	10.39	0.62	0.43	1.57	1.77	10.1	1.23
1968-69	35.08	12.77	2.46	2.47	2.2	56.68	0.57	0.47	0.85	0.2	0.59	2.76	59.44	8.85	0.54	0.37	0.96	1.82	12.74	0.89
1969-70	43.3	12.7	2.98	2.97	2.53	66.32	0.75	0.34	0.52	0.22	0.65	2.59	68.91	10.64	0.66	0.51	1.01	1.25	11.21	0.94
1970-71	47.86	9.67	2.99	3.44	2.31	69.65	1.49	0.9	0.62	0.25	1.12	4.5	74.15	12.34	0.65	0.53	0.78	1.44	9.47	1.59
1971-72	47.17	11.4	2.28	2.94	2.65	69.12	1.33	0.76	0.42	0.25	0.92	3.8	72.92	13.11	0.56	0.39	1.66	2.05	11.81	1.39
1972-73	42.56	12.3	1.8	2.92	2.21	64.08	0.65	0.8	0.38	0.18	0.91	2.99	67.07	9.98	0.53	0.29	1.13	1.63	11.08	0.85
1973-74	55.83	12.91	3.65	4.2	2.74	82.74	1.38	0.85	0.39	0.2	1.04	3.95	86.69	13.76	1.21	0.39	3.28	2.37	11.9	1.36
1974-75	57.0	15.71	3.08	4.84	3.18	86.68	1.27	0.86	0.46	0.28	1.19	4.18	90.86	14.13	1.15	0.46	4.56	1.59	12.98	1.28
1975-76	64.51	10.2	3.51	4.98	3.7	90.07	1.39	0.84	0.44	0.37	1.07	4.21	94.28	11.19	0.21	0.26	2.39	1.3	11.11	1.34
1976-77	49.3	10.65	2.45	3.01	3.08	71.24	1.68	0.64	0.24	0.24	0.64	3.52	74.76	5.83	0.41	0.23	2.61	1.33	11.29	0.59
1977-78	56.05	14.33	3.78	4.74	3.53	86.52	1.36	0.5	0.3	0.21	0.85	3.33	89.85	10.23	0.4	0.28	2.17	2.63	13.42	1.0
1978-79	74.32	14.18	3.58	3.6	3.43	102.6	1.5	0.98	0.45	0.16	0.88	4.06	106.67	11.6	0.43	0.25	3.48	1.91	10.06	2.03
1979-80	63.07	16.56	2.95	3.94	2.65	92.0	0.86	0.92	0.49	0.19	0.74	3.28	95.28	11.19	0.43	0.25	4.5	1.55	9.35	1.76
1980-81	70.11	10.82	3.36	7.25	2.45	95.77	1.83	1.07	0.44	0.14	0.61	4.14	99.91	8.6	0.26	0.31	4.89	1.64	10.42	1.49

Contd.

Years	Rice	Jowar	Bajra	Maize	Ragi	Total cereals	Green gram	Black gram	Red gram	Bengal gram	Horse gram	Total Pulses	Total food grains	Ground nut	Castor	Sesa-mum	Cotton	Tobacco	Sugar cane	Chillies
1981-82	78.68	13.34	4.44	6.32	2.87	109.5	2.09	0.9	0.6	0.24	0.78	4.68	114.15	14.37	0.57	0.29	6.63	1.93	16.43	1.65
1982-83	76.71	15.2	2.6	7.44	2.34	105.9	2.86	1.26	0.45	0.26	0.96	5.85	111.73	11.33	0.68	0.26	6.24	2.7	13.45	1.92
1983-84	87.91	11.25	3.61	5.22	2.62	113.2	2.45	1.32	0.74	0.23	0.82	5.66	118.81	17.16	0.66	0.27	10.19	1.86	10.38	1.79
1984-85	69.09	12.16	2.06	4.33	2.16	91.13	1.73	1.9	0.56	0.17	0.61	5.02	96.15	12.58	0.56	0.25	9.84	1.71	10.08	2.53
1985-86	76.13	11.62	2.1	4.14	2.06	97.45	2.42	2.14	0.85	0.17	0.64	6.29	103.74	13.11	0.55	0.32	7.43	1.46	9.97	3.23
1986-87	65.91	9.94	1.96	4.59	1.82	85.46	1.49	3.04	0.8	0.15	0.62	6.17	91.63	13.08	0.48	0.31	6.09	1.52	8.34	2.79
1987-88	70.87	11.46	1.56	5.33	1.69	92.43	2.28	3.02	0.45	0.19	0.53	6.57	99.0	19.06	0.72	0.22	5.37	1.05	9.89	2.51
1988-89	106.2	6.13	1.97	4.91	1.71	122.1	1.36	3.96	0.7	0.25	0.35	6.92	129.0	21.7	0.7	0.18	5.66	1.86	11.83	3.25
1989-90	99.59	9.02	1.82	6.7	2.08	120.9	1.42	3.76	0.78	0.37	0.41	6.82	127.72	20.82	0.85	0.15	9.31	2.03	12.16	4.01
1990-91	96.54	8.51	1.68	6.46	1.91	116.3	1.37	3.66	0.74	0.57	0.51	6.96	123.3	22.67	0.87	0.33	11.1	1.87	13,26	3.47
1991-92	92.49	6.66	1.35	6.35	1.52	109.1	2.19	3.41	1.19	0.47	0.54	7.92	117.05	21.52	0.92	0.41	12.99	2.57	15.16	2.6
1992-93	87.92	9.09	1.28	8.56	1.6	109.2	2.26	3.48	0.75	0.28	0.51	7.39	116.58	19.65	0.67	0.38	11.47	2.37	12.43	3.73
1993-94	95.62	8.73	1.11	7.76	1.63	115.8	2.18	2.41	1.04	0.65	0.4	6.77	122.54	25.46	0.75	0.4	13.49	1.88	14.18	3.23
1994-95	92.77	6.42	1.07	8.58	1.72	111.1	1.65	2.2	0.99	1.36	0.44	6.73	117.84	16.7	0.93	0.32	14.26	1.65	16.54	3.48
1995-96	90.14	6.49	1.27	8.76	1.48	109	1.91	3.52	1.02	0.71	0.44	7.72	116.67	26.26	0.71	0.54	16.1	1.7	15.61	3.64
1996-97	106.9	6.27	1.22	11.9	1.48	128.4	2.31	3.27	1.38	0.9	0.49	8.46	136.82	20.45	0.66	0.4	18.78	1.84	13.79	5.62
1997-98	85.1	5.15	0.67	10.83	0.9	103.1	1.34	2.15	0.57	0.59	0.44	5.16	108.22	11.56	0.42	0.16	13.2	2.02	13.46	3.38
1998-99	118.8	5.23	1.19	13.84	1.22	140.8	2.17	2.61	1.71	1.3	0.36	8.26	149.05	21.55	0.45	0.38	15.22	2.46	17.87	5.25
1999-00	106.4	5.36	0.97	14.73	1.11	129	2.11	2.95	1.55	0.95	0.36	8.01	136.98	10.89	0.58	0.38	15.79	1.93	19.67	4.96
2000-01	124.6	6.19	1.48	15.81	1.2	149.7	1.84	3.91	2.19	2.29	0.2	10.54	160.28	21.43	1.37	0.37	16.63	0.88	18	5.26
2001-02	113.9	6.34	0.71	14.57	1.03	137	1.55	3.83	1.88	3.63	0.39	11.38	148.36	12.5	0.83	0.27	18.77	1.68	17.67	5.91
2002-03	73.27	6.07	0.57	14.86	0.78	95.92	1.18	3.76	1.5	2.82	0.29	10.63	106.55	8.2	0.86	0.18	10.86	1.68	13.92	4.09
2003-04	89.53	7.42	1.48	24.77	1.01	124.6	3.12	2.0	2.18	4.57	0.39	12.39	136.97	9.86	1.32	0.43	18.9	1.96	15.04	7.97
2004-05	96.01	5.16	0.81	20.64	0.87	123.8	1.6	2.59	2.19	3.45	0.26	10.17	133.94	16.39	1.05	0.38	21.9	1.66	15.73	7.48
2005-06	117.0	5.88	0.82	30.87	0.79	155.8	1.65	2.5	3.01	6.27	0.21	13.75	169.5	13.66	1.4	0.29	21.08	1.98	18.65	5.38

Source: Directorate of Economics and Statistics, A.P.

the 1970's and the achievement of self-sufficiency was accorded high priority in policy. India achieved self sufficiency in food grains in the 1970s and has sustained it. Since then, it improved its capacity to cope up with year-to-year fluctuations in food production. The achievement of macro food grain security at the national level did not percolate down to households and chronic food insecurity in India still is high.

The challenges involved in ensuing food and nutrition security relate to both the production and distribution of food. Inequitable distribution rather than inadequate production, is the major factor underlying India's current problem of malnutrition. The inequality cannot be corrected through exercises in tokenism and populist 'give away' programmes but only through creation of and support to income generating skills among the poor.[17]

As observed by C. H. Hanumantha Rao, though per capita demand for foodgrains has declined, it has to do more with diversification of food consumption. Food security should not be confused with foodgrain security. Though, food stocks are embarrassingly large, they give the confidence that foodgrains can tide over any drought without having to import foodgrains. They also provide resources to carry out anti-poverty programmes[18]. In India, edible oils are a significant source of essential fats. However, fat intake is almost absent among the rural poor, for whom edible oils are largely unaffordable. Edible oil consumption should be encouraged among the rural poor by supply via PDS[19].

Food self-sufficiency or food security is usually measured in terms of calories. Through an analysis of the Indian nutritional supply and accessibility, Bruno Dorin focuses on the determining factors of production, distribution and consumption of lipids. He demonstrates that there is a much more severe deficiency of fats (and of calories) than that of carbohydrates and proteins especially in rural India. This leads to assess the role of food (grain) policies following the green revolution[20]. It may be said that the food insecurity in India is determined by an unequal distribution of lipids rather than by an unequal distribution of carbohydrates and proteins[21].

Food Intake, Calorie Intake and Nutritional Status

The relationship between food intake and nutritional status is not that close. Professor Sukhatme, in his various studies on malnutrition explained that the conversion efficacy of food into energy depends upon an individual's access to safe drinking water, health care and environmental hygiene. The complexity of the connection between calorie intake and nutrition status is dramatized by Kerala that had, and continues to have, the lowest calorie intake but also the lowest incidence of severe malnutrition among children and adolescents, and chronic energy deficiency (BMI<18.5) among adults. Also remarkable is the fact that Kerala, which continues to be at the bottom of the ranking by calorie intake at levels far below recommended levels, has recorded the largest improvements in the nutrition indicators[22].

Emerging Trends in the Consumption of Food Stuffs

The data from NSSO 43 & 49/50 Rounds indicate that there has been a small reduction in cereal and pulse consumption and an increase in milk and edible oil consumption among rural population.

National Nutrition Monitoring Bureau (NNMB) data on consumption of cereals and other foodstuffs along with the Recommended Dietary Intake (RDI) has been given in the Table 4.

Table 3
Consumption of Food Stuffs in Rural India
(Consumption per person in kgs/month)

Item	*1987-88*	*1993-94*
Cereals	14.40	13.40
Pulses	0.25	0.24
Edible oil	0.33	0.37
Milk	3.20	3.94

Data on time trends in food intake in rural areas from NNMB surveys shows that over the last three decades there has been some decline in cereal consumption in rural areas.

Table 4
Average Consumption of Foodstuffs (gms/cu/day) in Rural Areas

Foodstuff	*RDI*	*1975-79*	*1988-90*	*1995-96*	*2000-01*
Coarse cereals	460	505	490	450	457
Milk & Milk Products	150	116	92	85	85
Pulses	40	34	32	29	34
Roots & Tubers	50	13	23	24	25
Green Leafy Vegetables	40	8	9	15	18
Other Vegetables	60	54	49	47	57
Fats & Oils	20	14	13	12	14
Sugar & Jaggery	30	23	29	21	23

Source: NNMB reports

Over this period there has been a substantial improvement in availability of cereals. The decline is therefore not due to economic constraints. Over the same period there has been a decline in the consumption of pulses, which are a major source of protein in Indian diets. This is partly attributable to the soaring cost of pulses and inability of the poor to purchase adequate pulses inspite of higher expenditure on pulses. In spite of massive increase in milk output in the country, there has not been any improvement in per capita consumption of milk over years. Consumption of vegetables and fruits also continues to be very low. In rural areas there has not been any significant increase in percapita consumption of fats and oils and sugar and jaggery. Data from NNMB surveys suggest that dietary intake has not undergone any major increase in consumption of fat/oils, sugar and processed food. There has not been any increase in energy intake. These data are confirmed by the consumer expenditure on food items reported by the NSSO.

There has been some decline in intake of most of the nutrients in rural areas over the last three decades. A reduction in percent of total energy intake from carbohydrates and some increase in percent dietary energy from fats have occurred over the past three decades. In spite of this, the proportion of dietary energy from fat remains lower than 15 percent. Dietary intake of iron in Indian dietaries has always been low. The steep decline in iron intake reported in the last NNMB survey can be attributed to different estimation methods, which showed that absorbable iron was 50 percent less compared to earlier values.

Table 5
Nutrient Intake in Rural Areas
(consumption unit /day)

Nutrient	*RDI*	*1975-79*	*1988-90*	*1995-96*	*2000-01*
Energy (Kcal)	2425	2340	2283	2108	2255
Protein (g)	60	62.9	61.81	53.7	58.7
Calcium (mg)	400	590	556	521	523
Iron (mg)	28	30.2	28.4	24.9	17.5
Vitamin A (mcg)	600	257	294	300	242
Thiamin (mg)	1.2	1.6	1.5	1.2	1.4
Riboflavin (mg)	1.4	0.9	0.9	0.9	0.8
Niacin (mg)	16	15.7	15.5	12.7	17.1
Vitamin C (mg)	40	37	37	40	51
Folic acid (mg)	100	-	-	153	62

Source: NNMB reports

Consumption of various livestock products in India has increased considerably over the last two decades. Per capita consumption of eggs has been increased by one-and-half times. Growth in per capita consumption of meat and fish was relatively low. A strong positive relationship exists between income and per capita consumption of livestock products. With sustained growth in rural incomes and reduction in poverty, demand for livestock products is expected to increase faster. This implies a need for a faster growth in production of livestock products. At present, productivity of Indian livestock is low compared to the world average. Average milk yield of Indian bovines is about 50% of the world average, and mutton yield is about 70% and pork yield is about 50% indicating that there is a considerable scope to raise the production through yield improvement measures. The emerging trends in meat consumption imply that the structure of meat production will gradually shift towards monogastrics (poultry and pig) with the rising per capita incomes. (Table 6)

Table 6
Trends in the Annual Per Capita Consumption of Livestock Products in India

(kg/person/year)

Commodity	*1980*	*1990*	*2000*
Meat	3.7	4.5	4.5
Egg	0.7	1.2	1.5

Food and Nutritional Security Programmes and Strategies to improve Dietary Intake and Nutritional Status: Strategies to improve Dietary Intake and Nutritional Status include adequate agricultural production of cereals, pulses, vegetables and other food stuffs needed to fully meet the requirement of growing population, improvement in purchasing power through employment generation and employment assurance schemes, providing subsidized food grains through TPDS to the families below poverty line (BPL), explore feasibility of providing subsidized coarse grains to families BPL. Government interventions to ensure food and nutrition provisioning can be broadly classified into: (a) subsidised distribution of foodgrains, (b) nutrition provision through Anganwadis, and (c) Food for Work programme. The Public Distribution System (PDS) and the Integrated Child Development Services (ICDS), are by far the most important public interventions in terms of their objectives and coverage.

Targeted Public Distribution System (TPDS)

Foodgrains are allotted every month for distribution to the BPL families at a fixed price. As part of the TPDS, two major schemes, namely, the Antyodaya Anna Yojana and Annapurna Scheme have been launched with the purpose of nutritional support both at the household and individual levels. The Antyodaya Anna Yojana was introduced in December 2001 and is targeted at the ultrapoor and destitute households as identified by the Gram Panchayats and Gram Sabhas/Pallie sabhas. The basis of targeting under this Scheme is superior to income-based identification, which leaves ample room for false inclusion of the non-poor. This is important since the rate of subsidy involved under this scheme is much higher than that under the PDS. The Annapurna Scheme, like the Antyodaya Anna Yojana, is a component of the TPDS. This Scheme seeks to provide direct nutritional support to indigent senior citizens by entitling them to 10 kg. of free grain per month.

Targeted Nutritional Interventions

While the above programmes aim at improving physical and economic access to staple food and thereby provide indirect nutritional support. Direct nutritional support programmes are typically targeted towards certain sections of the population, who are vulnerable to nutritional stress and involve in-kind transfers. The ICDS is the most important nutritional support programme and is now focused in regions with high incidence of poverty. Unlike the PDS, ICDS is an in-kind income transfer programme, which integrates supplementary nutrition with primary health care and informal education. The target groups of ICDS include children in the age group 0–6 years, pregnant women, and lactating mothers from the poorer sections of the population in rural areas as well as in some urban slums. The ICDS is the most cost-effective among all income transfer programmes. With its vast network at the village level, it has the ability to protect the most vulnerable sections of the population from nutritional stress, both acute and chronic.

Another important scheme, namely, the Pradhan Mantri Gramodaya Yojana (PMGY) was introduced by the Government of India during 2000–01 in place of the Basic Minimum Services Programme. Under PMGY, nutritional support in the shape of supplementary feeding of malnourished children less than 3 years of age is a very important component.

The Jawahar Rozgar Yojana (JRY) and Employment Assurance Scheme (EAS) have been merged into one scheme, called the Sampoorna Grameen Rozgar Yojana (SGRY). This is a programme of rural employment generation along with a food transfer component and has the potential of making a dent on chronic poverty and food insecurity at the household level by providing direct nutritional support and increasing purchasing power.

NEED FOR THE STUDY

Promoting healthy diets requires a multi-sectoral approach involving various relevant sectors in societies. Agricultural and food sector must be given due importance in any consideration for promotion of healthy diets for individuals and population groups. Food strategies must not merely be directed at ensuring food security for all, but must also achieve the consumption of adequate quantities of safe and good quality food that together make up a healthy diet. Any recommendation to that effect will have implications for all components in the food chain. It is therefore useful at this juncture to examine trends in consumption patterns and deliberate on the potential of the food and agriculture sector to meet the demand and challenges. Intake of calorie, protein, fats per diem per consumer unit, distribution of intake of nutrients over different food groups, distribution of households/persons over different calorie intake levels; number of meals taken by households during a day etc., forms the base for nutritional and dietary analysis. The dietary changes that characterize the "nutrition transition" include both quantitative and qualitative changes in the diet. Data on the national availability of the main food commodities provide a valuable insight into diets and their evolution over time. Although such average per capita supplies are derived from national data, they may not correspond to actual per capita availability, which is determined by many other factors such as inequality in access to food. Likewise, these data refer to "average food available for consumption", which, for a number of reasons (for example, waste at the household level), is not equal to average food intake or average food consumption. Actual food availability may vary by region, socioeconomic level and season. Based on national data, such averages do not provide information on the distribution of food within communities and households. Per capita intake of calorie and protein based on the averages does not say much about the real nutritional situation of household. It is more pertinent to ask, who is consuming how much? This perhaps cannot be answered with the available grouped data. Even if household level data are available this generally ignores intra-household distribution. It is important to examine the extent of inter-household and intra-household inequality in food intake and nutritional status. A substantial amount of empirical work has been done in India on such welfare indicators as per capita income or expenditure and on the extent of inequality and poverty. But, not much work has been done on the behaviour of the intake of nutrition. The importance of irrigation in foodgrain production was well recognised and efforts during the past five decades enhanced the irrigation facilities for an appreciable extent. But, still differences exit in canal irrigated areas and tank irrigated areas where the availability of water depends on the rainfall. This inturn influences the food consumption pattern of the rural people who generally consume locally available and produced food products. Therefore, there is a need to conduct household level study in order to examine the food consumption difference and nutritional differences among the rural households.

OBJECTIVES

The specific Objectives of the Study are :

1. To examine the food intake and nutritional status of the rural households of Andhra Pradesh based on the NSSO data.
2. To measures the inter-household and intra-household difference in the food intake and consumption pattern of the canal irrigated and rain-fed agricultural villages.
3. To measure the inter-household and intra-household differences in the nutritional status of the canal irrigated and rain-fed agricultural villages and

4. To suggest the policy measures for the improvement of the food intake, consumption pattern and nutritional status of the rural households.

METHODOLOGY

Sample Design

Three-stage simple random sampling method has been adopted for the Study. In the first stage, two rural mandals from each district was selected. In the second stage two villages namely Repuru from Kakinada rural mandal of East Godavari District and Gutchimi from Seethanagaram mandal of Vizianagaram District were selected. Initially, a census of all households was carried out for the selected villages during January 2007. Based on the village census data, the sample households for detailed survey was enlarged to make it representative and proportional to the number of households. From the canal irrigated village, 204 sample households and from rain-fed village, 124 sample households were randomly selected which is 25% of the total households of the villages. Total households of the selected villages are 817 and 493 respectively, for canal irrigated and rain-fed villages.

Database

The Study is based on both primary and secondary data. The secondary data on nutritional status and food intake relating to Andhra Pradesh were taken from various surveys of National Sample Survey Organisation. Discussions have been carried out with the District officials who were associated with the planning, for collecting information about various mandals and villages. For collecting the primary data, sample survey method is adopted. Pre-tested, structured questionnaires were administered to collect information on socio-economic factors, sources of food availability, food intake, food preparation and related aspects from the sample households. Data regarding food frequency, and intake were collected with the help of questionnaires and interviews. Food consumption patterns were recorded by a 24-hour recall method.

Survey Period

The primary data collected pertain to the period from April 2007 to May 2007 when generally the temperatures are high. This period was taken to reduce the influence of seasonal variations in availability of food for consumption which has it own impact on the household food consumption pattern and nutritional value food.

Statistical Techniques

The concepts used in order to calculate the nutritional issues are followed from NSSO surveys. The nutritional intake of a sample household has been measured by converting the quantities of the items of food consumed by the household into equivalent amounts of energy, protein and fat.

The data are analysed by various statistical tools. The conventional techniques such as percentages, averages and ratios were used to analyse and compare the various sources of food and consumption patterns for the two types of villages. The nature of inequality has been assessed by comparing the values of mean, standard deviation and skewness of various food items. For easy understanding of the inequalities in the energy consumption, graphical presentation was also done by using histograms.

In order to study the nature and extent of inequality of energy consumption, Gini ratios were computed. In order to measure the extent of inequalities in nutritional status, or in other words, under-nutrition, the formula for Sen's Index of Poverty is converted as Index of under-nutrition U.

The following formula is used:

$$U= q \mid (z - m) (1-G_{ni}) \mid / z^{*}n$$

Where

'U' is index of under-nutrition

'q' is number of people below the calorie norm

'z' is calorie norm[23]

'm' is the mean level of calorie intake

'n' is the total sample population

'G_{ni}' is the Gini Co-efficient of the distribution of calorie intake among the sample households.

ORGANISATION OF THE STUDY

The Study is organized into seven chapters. The introductory chapter presents the research problem, need for the Study, specific objectives of the Study, methodology followed, techniques used and chapterisation of the Study.

The second chapter presents the review of literature and the gaps in the existing literature.

Chapter three is divided into two sections. In the first section, the profile of the sample districts, and villages is presented. Second section presents the socio-economic profile of the sample households.

Chapter four presents the food intake and nutritional status of AP the rural population based on the estimates of NSSO in various rounds.

The Chapter five examines the difference in food intake among various social and occupational groups. It also measures the intra-household and inter-household differences in consumption pattern of various food items.

Chapter six examines the nutritional status of the sample households in terms of calorie, protein and fat per consumer unit per diem. It also measures the intra-household and inter-household inequalities among the rural people of the canal irrigated and rain-fed agricultural villages.

The major findings of the study and policy implications are presented in the last Chapter.

FOOTNOTES

1. V.S. Vyas (2005): " From Elimination of Hunger to Food and Nutrition Security: Performance, Prospects and Policy Options in Selected Asian Countries", in Food Security in Asian Countries, Ed., by Vijay S Vyas, Academic Foundation, Asian Development Research Forum, and International Development Research Centre, p.23.

2. WHO (2003): Global and Regional Food Consumption Patterns and Trends.
3. V S Vyas (2005): op. cit., p. 17
4. Lawrence Haddad, Christine Peña, Chizuru Nishida, Agnes Quisumbing, and Alison Slack (1996): Food Security and Nutrition Implications of Intra-household Bias: A Review of Literature, Food Consumption and Nutrition Division, International Food Policy Research Institute, Discussion Paper No. 19.
5. Chatterjee, M (1995): Distributing the loans seminar 433 September.
6. Gopalan, C (1989): 'Science and Nutrition in the future' plenary lecture, XVI International Congress of Nutrition.
7. Abusaleh Shariff Ananta C. Mallick: Dynamies of food intake and Nutrition by expenditure class in India, Economic and Political Weekly, XXXIV, No.27.
8. Government of India (2002): Agriculture Statistics at a glance 2002, Ministry of Agriculture, New Delhi.
9. Government of India (2002): Report of Department of Economics and Statistics 2002, Ministry of Agriculture, New Delhi.
10. Allen Lindsay H and Christopher P Howson (1995): Estimated Mean per capita Energy requirements for planning emergency food Aid Rations, National Academy Press Washington. D.C.
11. P. Kumar (1998): "Food Demand & Supply Projections for India", *Agricultural Economics Policy Paper 98-01*, IARI, New Delhi.
12. Institute for Human Development (2000): India Water Vision 2025, Report of the Vision Development Consultation.
13. Madhusudan Bhattarai and A. Narayanamoorthy (2004): "Irrigation Impact On Agricultural Growth And Poverty Alleviation: Macro Level Impact Analyses In India", Water Policy Research, International Water Management Institute (IWMI– TATA), Gujarat.
14. B.D. Dhawan (1989): Studies in Irrigation and Water Management, Commonwealth Publishers, New Delhi.
15. Government of Andhra Pradesh: Strategy Paper on Irrigation Development, *http://www.aponline.gov.in/*
16. Government of Andhra Pradesh: Revitalising Agriculture, http://www.aponline.gov.in/
17. C Gopalan (1995): Towards food and Nutrition Security: *Economic and Political Weekly*, Vol. XXX, No. 52, December 30, pp. A-134 to A-141.
18. C. H. Hanumantha Rao (2005): Agriculture, food Security, Poverty and Environment: eassys on Post-Reform India, Oxford University press, New Delhi.
19. G. Aneeja, (2001): Edible Oil Consumption Need for change in Rural India: *Economic and Political Weekly*, Vol. XXXVI, No. 38, September 22, pp.3595-3597.
20. Bruno Dorin (1999): Food Policy and Nutritional Security: Unequal Access to Lipids in India: *Economic and Political Weekly*, Vol. XXXIV, No. 26, June 26, pp. 1709-1717.

21. NIN (1989): Nutritive values of India Foods, National Institute of Nutrition, Hyderabad, p. 156.
22. Dr. C. Rangarajan (2005): Dimensions of Nutrition Security, Meeting on Food and Nutrition Security in South Asia, Inaugural address, Nutrition Foundation of India, New Delhi.
23. See Appendix 3

2

REVIEW OF LITTERATURE

STUDIES BASED ON SECONDARY DATA

The study on 'Inter-Regional Variations in Calorie Intake' by P G K Panikar[1] (1980) was based on the estimates of calorie intake by National Sample Survey Organisation in various rounds. The Study mainly focused on the reasons for the fall in calorie intake during '70s in India despite an increase in per capita production of cereals and the reasons for the inter-state variations. The Study inferred that the level of calorie intake is a function of their income, level of employment, and the prices of cereals, which in turn, are determined by the level of production and the composition of the cereal basket.[2]

Rajaram Dasgupta attempted to estimate the intake of nutrients, calorie, protein, calcium, iron and vitamin A in different states at different time points. The Study used NSS data and NIN data for the analysis. The Study found that intake of vitamin and calcium along with that of calories are too meager. There is practically no expenditure clause where average intakes of Calcium and vitamin A are more than the recommended level. NIN data, too, indicate that deficiency regarding vitamin A calorie, protein and iron intakes in general, are much less. There is a deficiency of iron intake among pregnant women. The Study also found that income is the major factor influencing intake of nutrients. Per capita intake of calories and percapita production of cereals are positively correlated. Per capita production of cereals and per capita consumption of cereals show a good correlation, if the latter be expressed as a quadratic function of the former. This shows that, increase of per capita production of cereals is an indicator of rise in income, consumption of cereals first increases but later expenditure is diverted to non-cereal items. Intakes of calorie and protein increased with the size of landholdings. They are least among landless labourers. So far as time trend is concerned, it is definite that the calorie intake deteriorated during sixties and seventies. Per capita intake decreased, but no such trend emerges during three years i.e. 1971-72, 1972-73 and 1973-74. The inequality in real income seems to have increased between sixties and seventies, as the gap in share of calorie from cereals and substitutes in all states, and also the gap in calories intake in quite a few states between different expenditure groups have widened between 1961-62 and 1971-72.

The Study by Rajaram Dasgupta[3] (1984) on Nutritional Situation in India aimed at examining the average intake of calorie and protein and the size distribution of such intake across the population in different states. The Study also estimated in inter-state inequality in intake of nutrients. The Study used Gini co-efficient measure and the index of undernutrition to estimate the inequalities in the calorie intake. The Study found that nutritional inequality is more in rural areas than in urban areas, while index of undernutrition is less in rural areas.

An attempt is made in a study by C. Gopalan[4] in the (1995) to examine the status of different states with respect to their levels of nutritional status and 'social development' using data from NNMB and NFHS. The Study points out that the migration of rural population to urban areas introduces new dimensions to the food/nutrition problem.

To analyse the calorie deprivation in rural India during 1983-2000, JV Meenakshi and Brinda Vishwanathan[5] conducted a study in 2003. The analysis is based on household level data from the consumer expenditure surveys conducted by the NSSO for the years 1983 and 1999-2000, in 38th and 55th rounds of the NSS. The Study found that between 1983 and 1999-2000, the incidence of calorie deprivation in rural India would appear to have increased in most states. The depth and severity of calorie deprivation has declined in many states when k cal 2200 or lower norm is used and in all states if the median is used.

The Study conducted by Prema Ramachandran[6] (2004) was based on the NFHS-II (National Family Health Survey). It shows that eventhough breast-feeding is nearly universal, a substantial proportion of infants get breast-milk substitutes from three months of age. On the other hand, nearly two-third of infants does not receive semi-solid supplements even as late as nine months. This is a major non-economic factor responsible for under nutrition in early childhood, and should be corrected through intensive nutrition education aimed at bringing about changes in infant feeding and caring practices. National Nutrition Monitoring Bureau's (NNMB) data indicated that over this period there has been a substantial decline in severe grades of under nutrition in children. This might be due to better access to health care, thus reducing the adverse impact of infection on nutritional status, and better access to contraception and consequent decline in under nutrition associated with high parity. However, the decline in mild and moderate under nutrition has been relatively slow. Screening for detection of under nutrition and management through appropriate health and nutrition interventions has not yet been operationalised as a part of the ICDS Programme. The proportion of families where preschool children receive inadequate intake while adults have an adequate intake has nearly doubled. Data indicate that one of the major reasons for under nutrition in young children is faulty child feeding practices. Nutrition education to the family needs to impart that young children have a very low stomach capacity and in order to ensure adequate dietary intake, it is important to feed them once every four hours or even more often, may go a long way in reducing the prevalence of under nutrition in young children. Data from NFHS-II showed the poorest in Kerala have under nutrition rates comparable to the richest in UP. Data from the NNMB repeat surveys show that there has not been any substantial increase in the dietary intake of adolescents though there has been some improvement in height, weight and Body Mass Index (BMI) between 1975-79 and 1995-97. Data from NNMB also show that there has been some increase in obesity among adolescents, especially in the affluent groups both in urban and rural areas. However, the prevalence of micronutrient deficiencies continues to be high. Nutrition education programmes need to be undertaken on a large scale.

Ramesh Golait and N.C. Pradhan[7] (2004) observed the changing food consumption pattern in rural India and the implication of that on food and nutrition security, by using the data from 43rd, 55th and 57th rounds of NSSO. They observed that there is a marked decline in the consumption of all the cereal items over the period 1987-88 through 2001-02 in almost all states both in rural and urban areas. However, malnutrition and under-nutrition occurs in many families that are not poor– because people do not always know what food or consumption practices are best for them.

Praduman Kumar, Mruthyunjaya and Madan M Dev[8] (2007) analyzed the long-term changes in Indian food basket and nutrition with the help of 38th and 55th rounds of NSS. The Study found that the food consumption pattern in India is diversifying towards high value commodities like vegetable oils, fruits, vegetables, milk and eggs. The decline in per capita consumption of cereals, in particular, coarse, has worsened the nutritional status of the rural poor.

Ranjan Ray[9] in his study examined the changes in the nature and quantity of food consumption in India during the reforms decade of the 1990s, and analysed their implications for calorie intake and undernourishment. The Study documented the decline in cereal consumption, especially in the urban areas, and provides evidence that suggests an increase in the prevalence of undernourishment over the period, 1987/88– 2001/2002. The results also point to a significant number of households, even in the top expenditure decile, suffering from under nourishment. This calls for a reassessment of the current strategy of directing the Targeted

Public Distribution System (TPDS) exclusively at households "below the poverty line" (BPL). This Study shows that, both as a source of subsidised calories and as a poverty reducing instrument, the PDS is of much greater importance to the female headed households than it is to the rest of the population. Another important result is that, notwithstanding the sharp decline in their expenditure share during the 1990s, rice and wheat continue to provide the dominant share of calories, especially for the rural poor. The Indian experience is in sharp contrast to that in Vietnam which witnessed a large increase in calorie intake and, consequently, a decrease in the prevalence of under-nourishment in the late 1990s. The Vietnamese diet displayed increased diversification during the 1990s with a greater role for protein rich animal products and a more balanced diet of nutrients than in India.

STUDIES BASED ON PRIMARY DATA

Amartya Sen, and Sunil Sengupta[10] examined the malnutrition of rural children and sex bias in the year1983. The Study reports empirical field work done by the authors at Agro-Economic Research Centre at Santiniketan. The studies of nutritional conditions of children below 5 years of age in the two villages of Sahajapur and Kuchli provide firm evidence of: (1) remarkable high incidence of under nourishment, even of severe and disastrous types and (2) systematic sex bias reflected in higher deprivation of girls vis-à-vis boys. The sex bias is reflected both in: (1) greater prevalence of under nourishment of various degrees among girls than among boys, and (2) lower growth dynamics of girls vis-à-vis boys. Interestingly enough the village with better overall nutrition record has much sharper sex discrimination. The economic benefits accruing to the children of Kuchli through land reform, etc, seem to have primarily benefited boys vis-à-vis girls. The performance of girls in terms of nutritional criteria are broadly similar in the two villages, and it is the better position of boys in Kuchli that seems to make both the average nutritional record of Kuchli noticeably higher and also the extent of sex bias clearly greater. The authors discussed possible influences operating on the two villages which may throw light on the various contrasts between them as well as some policy issues related to the respective roles of land reform and direct nutritional intervention.

Cowan and Dhano[11] in conducted a study in 1983 in Rural Punjab on individual food consumption of the children (2-3 years old). The Study based on the primary data collected from home visits by adopting two-day recall method. The Study found that more than three times as many girls than boys from privileged families are malnourished. Twice as many girls as boys from underprivileged families were reported as undernourished.

Pettigrew[12] conducted a study in Punjab during 1986 to observe the breast feeding and weaning practices of mothers to assess the intra-household differences. The Study is based on a sample of 55 children from rich, average, and poor households. The data were collected through participant observation and home visits. The study found that boys were fed first in all types of households, although girls were breast-fed longer. In weaning, supplementary milk is not willingly supplied to girls, though it is more likely to be provided for boys. The level of income and ownership of land are important variables associated with child health. Labourer families contained five out of six children suffering from 3rd degree malnutrition and only two out of 18 healthy children.

The village level studies conducted by Behrman[13] in India during 1988 focused on the intra-household differences in the food and nutrient intake among the children in rural areas. The 24-hour recall method was adopted to collect the data. His studies indicate that during the surplus season, nutrients are distributed among children within a household, regardless of individual endowments. During the lean seasons, however, the measurement of inequality aversion is significantly reduced, rendering later-born and less well-endowed children more vulnerable when availability of nutrients is at lowest level. Standardised seasonal requirements do not differ significantly between boys and girls for calories, carotene, riboflavin, vitamin C, and calcium.

D. Hanumantha Rao, G.N.V. Brahman, K. Mallikharjuna Rao, Ch. Gal Reddy, and N. Pralhad Rao[14] conducted a study in Mysore District during 1993 to assess the nutritional status of 'Jenu Kurubas'–a primitive Tribe of Karnataka State. They randomly selected six villages and 1/5 of households in each village. They followed the 24-hour recall method to collect the diet data. The Study found that except for the green leafy vegetables, the intake of other food stuffs and average levels of nutrients were lower than the Recommended Dietary Allowance (RDA) norms.

Santosh Sangwan, Sudha Chhikara and Shakuntala Punia conducted a study on the factors affecting nutritional status of the rural infants in Haryana in the year 1993. The data were collected from purposively selected villages of District Hisar. A sample of 50 one year old rural male infants was selected randomly from the villages. The Study found that the nutritional status of an infant had no significant dependence on the birth order but had significant dependence on type of family, caste, occupation of the parents, education of the parents, land holdings and family income.

I.V. Parthasaradhy and K. Sheela[16] conducted a study in 1993 to assess the effect of public distribution system of food grains on consumption and nutritional status of the preschool children in the State of Karnataka. They selected a sample of 105 families, of which 35 having green card, 35 having red card and 35 card-less families, and having pre-school children. The nutritional status of the selected children was assessed by anthropometric indices. The Study found that the children of the card-less families suffered a deficiency of both calories and protein in the absence of food grain subsidy. Rationed food from PDS contributed considerable amount of calories in the household diet of children from green card and red card families and in turn improved the nutritional status of the children.

Dalip Kumar and T.M. Dak[17] studied on food security in Haryana State by using secondary as well as primary data. The Study found that despite the rapid growth in population during the last 20 years or more, the per capita availability of cereals, has increased from 663 grms in 1968-69 to 153 grams in 1988-89. Like wise, per capita availability of vegetables rose from 52.4 grams to 101.5 grams, fruits from 11.0 grams to 26.8 grams and oilseeds from 12.3 grams to 83.9 grams. However, per capita availability of gur/jaggery declined from 191.6 grams to 114.8 grams during the same period. Findings indicate that majority of respondents were secure with regard to consumption of cereals, milk and milk products and sugar/ jaggery. Insecurity was noticed in the consumption of pulses, vegetables, fruits and fats.

Ruby Sain[18] conducted a study in Birbhum District on Nutritional Status of Tribal Children. The Study explored the problem of nutrition and hunger among the "Santals"; a tribe living in three villages of Birbhum District. The Study found that of the total of three villages, 40 percent of malnourished are children of age-group 0-12 years. Nearly 40 percent of male children and 35 per cent of female children suffer from moderate degree of malnutrition, whereas 28 percent of male and 13 percent of female children suffer from acute malnutrition which requires immediate medical attention. More than 35 percent consume less than the minimum level of 2800 calories. Mortality of children between 0-12 years of age group shows that 76 percent of male and 80 percent of female children died within 0-48 months and mortality rate is higher for females among the tribal people. Finally, the Study states that untimely death and severe malnourishment are characteristic features of the child population in tribal villages of Birbhum district.

A study on nutritional status of the agricultural labour was conducted in the Thane District of Maharastra by Bombale S.M., Thakare R.P., Borude S.G., and Torane, S.R.[19] in the year 1995. The Study found that in all the adivasi and non-adivasi groups, the consumption of various food stuffs were less as compared to recommended levels. Per capita calorie intake was higher in non-adivasi labour groups as compared to adivasi labour groups. About 78 percent of calorie requirement was through cereals. In case of protein intake, it was found to be higher in land holder agricultural labourers as compared to their counterparts. Cereals were found to be the major source of calorie followed by flees foods and eggs (due to ample supply of fish).

Jayalakshmi N. and Neelakantan S.[20] examined the effect of socio-economic status on the consumption of food items and nutrients in the year 1995. The Study was conducted in a village near to Coimbatore city in Tamil Nadu. The family diet survey was carried out by 24 hour recall method for three consecutive days for each family. The Study found that the intake of pulses, milk, oils, and fat was significantly influenced by per capita income, educational status and social status. Consumption of greens and oils are negatively influenced by family size. Calorie intake was significantly influenced by these three variables whereas the intake of protein was influenced by per capita income alone. The Study states that this may be due to the consumption of quality foods by high income families.

S. Geetha[21] examined the nutritional status of slum children of Mumbai in 1996. The Study is based on a survey of 525 households in a slum settlement in Mumbai. The survey collected socio-economic information and anthropometric data on all children in the surveyed households who were five years of age or below. These anthropometric data included information on the height, weight and mid-arm circumference of each child. The Study attempted to identify the prevalence of under nutrition among children of the surveyed households. The Study found that high proportion of children, especially girls, in the slum community were undernourished. The Study suggested a systematic public action to improve the nutritional status of slum children and also civic amenities in the slum.

A K Rajula Devi[22] conducted a study 2001 on food, poverty and consumption among landless labour households in wet and dry rice regions of Tamil Nadu. The food intake of landless agricultural labour households was measured twice, to find variations between slack and peak seasons within and between wet and dry villages, the 'caste' differences in food intake between backward castes (BC's) and scheduled castes (SC's) were examined. Findings showed that the majority of sample households survived on cereals and had only one main meal per day, a stark indicator of food insecurity. Female-headed households were the most adversely affected 'poverty group' in the study villages irrespective of caste. The landless people's lack of basic needs (clothing, shelter, household equipment and health care) revealed much more of their utter destitution than conventional food intake·

N. Arlappa, N. Balakrishna, Sharad Kumar, G.N.V. Brahmam, K. Vijayaraghavan[23] conducted a study in the year 2003 on diet and nutritional status of the elderly in rural India. The main purpose of this study is to assess the current diet and nutritional status of the elderly population (60 years of age) in rural India. The data collected on food and nutrient intakes of communities during 1996-97 by the National Nutrition Monitoring Bureau in the eight states of India is utilized for the purpose of this Study. Dietary intakes of 922 elderly individuals were assessed by 24-hour recall, and anthropometric measurements were taken on 3,646 individuals. The results suggested that the consumption of a majority of foods except cereals and millets, and roots and tubers among the elderly of both sexes, and other vegetables among females, was below the recommended dietary allowances for Indians. The intakes of energy, total fat, calcium and thiamin in both sexes and protein intakes among females were comparable to the recommended levels for adults. The prevalence of chronic energy deficiency as assessed by body mass index was higher in the males, while the prevalence of obesity was higher among females.

The study conducted[24] for United Nations Committee on Nutrition in the year 2004 examines the effectiveness of the Integrated Child Development Service Programme in addressing the challenge of child under nutrition in India. It finds that although the ICDS Programme appears to be well-designed and well-placed to address the multidimensional causes of malnutrition in India, there are several mismatches between the design of Programme and its actual implementation that prevent it from reaching its potential. These include an increasing emphasis on the provision of supplementary feeding and preschool education to children aged four to six years, at the expense of other programme components that are crucial for combating persistent under nutrition; a failure to effectively reach children under three and ineffective targeting of the poorest states and those with the highest levels of under nutrition which tend to have these lowest levels of programmes funding and coverage. In addition, ICDS faces substantial operational challenges. In India, approximately 60 million children are under weighted.

The study by Manu, N. Khetarpaul[25] in 2006 on food consumption pattern of Indian rural preschool children (four to five years) aimed to assess the food consumption pattern of 183 Indian preschool children in Fatehabad district of Haryana. Data regarding food frequency, myths and intake were collected with the help of questionnaires and structured interviews. Food consumption patterns were recorded using a 24-hour recall for three consecutive days. The food frequency pattern indicated that wheat was the most accepted cereal among almost all the families and the consumption of pulses was weekly or on alternate days. They consumed roots and tubers frequently but the consumption of green leafy vegetables, fruits and other vegetables depended on the availability only. Most of the families consumed buffalo's milk (93 per cent) and desi ghee (73 per cent) daily. More than half of the respondents' mothers believed bajra, maize (corn), some pulses, bathua (Chenopodium album) and fenugreek leaves, onion, garlic, ginger, desi ghee and sweets are hot foods. According to the 24-hour recall method for three consecutive days, the daily mean intake of all foodstuffs, namely, cereals, pulses, green leafy vegetables, roots and tubers, other vegetables, fruits, fats and oils, milk and milk products and sugar and jaggery was lower than their respective recommended dietary intake in the daily diets of preschool children.

Veera Kumari and R.K.P. Singh[26] examined the food security in rural Bihar in 2006 by conducting a village level survey. The Study envisages identifying the extent of food secured households along with their access to basic education, health facilities, and safe drinking water. The Study observed that the consumption level of cereals is higher than the Recommended Dietary Allowance in the study villages. However, the weaker section households are deficient in protective food items in their food basket.

Dr. Kaushik Bose, Dilip Bhunia, Ganesh Paul, Ashish Mukhopadhyay and Raja Chakraborty[27] conducted a community-based cross-sectional study to determine the magnitude of undernutrition among 549 school children (boys = 291 and girls = 258) aged 5-9 years of rural areas of East Midnapore district of West Bengal. The data were analyzed using the recommended indices of height-for-age (stunting) and weight-for-age (underweight) based on the NCHS standard. Prevalence of stunting (overall = 29.7%, boys = 29.6%, girls = 29.8%) and underweight (overall = 53.4%, boys = 54.6%, girls = 51.9%) was alarming among the children studied. There was no significant sex difference in nutritional status. Moreover, the age variations in stunting and underweight demonstrated similar age-trends for both sexes. Relative to undernutrition levels identified in other Third World countries, rural Bengalee children of the present study had very high rates. Thus, this Study provided evidence that undernutrition is still a leading problem among rural Bengalee primary school children of West Bengal and this has not improved in spite of nutrition intervention programmes which are currently in operation.

Maithili Ramachandran, K.S. Kavi Kumar and Brinda Viswanathan[28] attempted to analyse the determinants of chronic energy deficiencies based on a sample of ever-married women in the age group of 15-49 years in Uttar Pradesh (UP) in 1998-99. The results indicate that education, social infrastructure and quality of diet influence those who are likely to be CED in future, with significant rural urban differences. Apart from these well-known indicators, presence of drinking water source within the residence (whether piped or otherwise), women in the age group of 15-19 years, and education status of the husband seems important. More importantly, the results clearly highlight that the CED rates and vulnerability rates can be very different across two subgroups of population. Hence, the results from this Study would be more useful in targeting policy most effectively as the emphasis would now be on 'potential' deficient persons rather than on current ones, which is the convention in policy intervention.

STUDIES RELATING TO ANDHRA PRADESH

Pushpamma P, Geervani P, Rani MU[29], in 1982 undertook a study to investigate the food intake and nutrient adequacy of rural population in Andhra Pradesh, 280 families were covered. Dietary survey was conducted by a weighed method for estimating the food intake. Nutritional value of the food consumed was calculated. Nutritional status was assessed by anthropometry. Results were analysed for five age groups-preschool age, school age, adolescents, adults and people above 50 yr. The intake of green leafy vegetables, milk, animal protein foods and oils was very low in all age groups. The adequacy of energy ranged from 60 to 91 per cent, protein from 73 to 91 per cent, niacin from 52 to 84 per cent. The intake of vitamin A and ascorbic acid was grossly inadequate in every group. The nutritional status of school children and adolescents was less than the values reported for higher income group in the same region.

Jere R. Behrman and Anil B. Deolalikar[30] conducted a study in 1990 to assess the intra-household demand for nutrients in rural South India. In the Study they discussed three problems in standard estimates of these responses and then illustrated their implications for nutrient demand relations for a poor sample from rural south India. In the case of intra-household nutrient allocations, nutrient intakes for females systematically have lower price elasticities than for males, which may leave the females vulnerable at times of food shortages. Second problem related to unobserved fixed effects. In this case the study pointed out that not only the community fixed effects on which the previous literature has focused, but also household and individual fixed effects are important. Failure to control for them results in substantial upward biases in many estimated price responses. Third issue was use of current instead of permanent income, which *a priori* may account for the low estimated income elasticities. In this case, however, the Study found that the use of permanent income does not change the conclusion that the nutrient intakes responses to income are quite small.

Kupputhai U. and Mallika N.[31] conducted a study on nutritional status of adult women belonging to Khond, Gadaba and Porja Tribes of Andhra Pradesh in 1993. Out of the 11 mandals in Visakhapatnam District under Integrated Tribal Development Project, Paderu mandal was selected for conducting the study as this mandal had highest concentration of scheduled tribes than others. The study collected information on the anthropometric measurements such as height and weight of the selected women and calculated the Body Mass Index (BHg). The study found that the tribal women were living in a state of great deprivation due to poor socio-economic status. Anthropometric measurements showed that the weight deficits were maximum compared to height. BMI values indicated higher prevalence of mild forms of malnutrition. The food and nutrient intake of the tribal women were inadequate when compared with ICMR allowances and in general they were found to have a poor nutritional status.

B. Shantha Kumari and B. Sarada[32] conducted a study in 1993 on food and nutrient intake of vegetable growers' families. They selected two villages from Kovvur Mandal of West Godavri District of Andhra Pradesh to conduct the study. West Godavari district has more area under cultivation of vegetables. All the farmers in these two villages were enumerated. From the enumerated data, a total sample of 60 families representing 30 from each village, having at least one pre-school child were selected for the study. A comparative analysis is made between vegetable grower and non-vegetable grower families. The Study found that the consumption of protective foods was found to be significantly higher in the vegetable grower families compared to non-vegetable grower families. Food intake of families of vegetable growers and non-vegetable growers per consumer unit showed that the intake of cereals, other vegetables, milk and milk products were above the suggested allowances in both categories. But, it is significantly higher in vegetable grower families than non-vegetable grower families. The intake of protein and calcium were also higher in vegetable grower families than non-vegetable grower families.

P. Yasoda Devi and P. Geervani[33] conducted a study on determinants of nutrition status of rural preschool children in in 1994. A longitudinal study was conducted in four villages in Medak district of Andhra Pradesh. One-hundred and ninety-seven children up to four years old were selected from low-income households in the study area. Pre-tested, structured interviews were conducted to collect information on child-related, maternal, paternal, and socio-economic factors from the households. Two child-related factors, number of diarrhoeal episodes and calorie adequacy of diet, showed a highly significant effect on a child's current as well as past nutrition status. The results of this study indicate a strong influence of socio-economic status and parental care on the control of infectious diseases and food intake, which are the two major causes for malnutrition among children in developing countries.

P.Y.B. Reddy and A. Papa Rao[34] conducted a study to know the protein-calorie adequacy status among the sugalis, a large tribal population of pastoral nomads, inhabitating the Palakonda Hill ranges located in Cuddaph district of Andhra Pradesh in 1995. A sample of 200 families was selected to conduct the survey and 24 hour recall method was applied in order to assess the dietary pattern. The study found that majority of sugali males and females are deficient in protein and calories compared to ICMR Recommended Dietary Allowance. The inadequacy in both protein and calorie is high in females than in males.

Prameela Y., Chittemma Rao K. and Sarojini G,[35] in 1995, compared the nutritional status of the rural adolescent girls with that of the adolescent boys of the same families in Andhra Pradesh. They selected a sample of 300 adolescent girls and boys (150 each) from 11 to 18 years of age drawn from the rural areas of three regions of viz., Telangana, Rayalaseema and Coastal areas. Information on individual food intake was collected based on the 24 hour recall method. The study found that nutritional values were much closer to the ICMR standards for the boys than for girls. Among girls deficit in weight was more pronounced than that of height. Socio-economic factors of family size and birth order were found to negatively influence the nutritional status of the girls. The study states that it may be due to the discrimination against girls within the family especially among the lower socio-economic groups.

Khader V[36] conducted a study on food intake and nutrient adequacy of rural population of Guntur district of Andhra Pradesh, in 1996. The objective of the study was to investigate the food intake and nutrient adequacy of rural population. A total of 1200 pre-school children were covered under the study from three divisions of the district. A 3 day dietary survey was conducted by a weighed method for estimating the food intake. Nutritional value of the food consumed was calculated. Nutritional status was assessed by anthropometry. Consumption of milk was very inadequate. Most of the protein and energy were derived from cereals. It is also revealed that ascorbic acid and beta-carotene deficiency seem to be most predominant followed by riboflavin, thiamine, iron and niacin.

The study conducted by Schmid M.A., Egeland G.M., Salomeyesudas B., Satheesh P.V., Kuhnlein H.V.[37] in 2001 on traditional food consumption and nutritional status of Dalit mothers in rural Andhra Pradesh for 2007 aimed at to describe the prevalence of malnutrition and their correlates of nutrient and traditional food consumption in rural Dalit mothers. The study is based on the cross-sectional data, collected through socio-cultural questionnaires. Food frequency information was collected on 24-h recall method during both summer and rainy seasons. The sample consists of 220 Dalit mothers with young children from 37 villages in the Medak District. The study found that the prevalence of CED among mothers (body mass index < 18.5 kg/m[2]) was 58%. Illiterate women and active women were more likely to have CED than those literate and non-active (relative risks (RR) = 1.6 and 1.4, respectively, P≤0.05), but literacy and activity level were not significant in multivariable analyses including sanitation and number of children ≤5 years of age. Increasing levels of fat intake, as a percent of total energy, was significantly associated with lower risk of CED (RR of the lowest 25th percentile compared to those in the 75th percentile or above was 1.6, $P \leq 0.05$), findings that remained significant in multivariable analyses. Consumption of pulses (g/day) was also inversely related to CED in univariate and multivariable analyses. Carbohydrate intake, as a percent of total energy, was inversely related to percent energy from fat ($r=-0.96$, $P \leq 0.01$), and, although positively related to CED in univariate analyses, carbohydrate consumption was not significant in multivariable analyses. Mothers' age and income was positively related to vitamin A deficiency. The study concludes that CED and vitamin A malnutrition among Dalit women are predominant problems in this area. Increased consumption of local traditional Dalit food (particularly sorghum, pulses, vegetables and animal source food) should be incorporated as an important component of intervention strategies to improve nutritional status.

B. Sambi Reddy[38] analysed the food security in Andhra Pradesh in the context of subsidized rice scheme in 2004. The Study considered the data on production, procurement, and distribution of rice in Andhra Pradesh for the period of 1970-99. The government policy was also taken into consideration to assess the impact. The study employs regression technique. They estimated three regression equations $Y_1 = f(X, p)$, $Y_2 = f(X, p)$ and $Y_2 = f(Y_1, p)$, where X is production of rice, p is government policy, Y_1 is procurement of rice and Y_2 is distribution of rice. To assess the impact of 'subsidised rice scheme' on food (cereals) consumption levels in Andhra Pradesh the study used the NSSO's 50th round (1993-94) household consumer expenditure data. The study found that foodgrains production and per capita availability of grains in particular rice, has increased in the state mainly due to adoption of improved technology by the farmers. The procurement policy with minimum support price (MSP) on one hand and the enhanced demand for rice due to public distribution at subsidized price on the other hand motivated the farmers to increase production of rice in Andhra Pradesh. From the regression analysis it is conformed that the government policy i.e., introduction of 'Two-Rupee-Kilo Rice Scheme' enhanced the procurement and distribution quantities significantly. The food security measured in terms of per capita quantity consumption of cereals is improved in PDS beneficiary households due to public distribution of rice at subsidized price. The beneficiary category of households consumed higher quantities of rice and total cereals at less expenditure compared to non-beneficiary households. Also, the share of expenditure on non-food items in former category of households was more than the latter. The study confirms that a committed PDS enhances production and procurement and acts as an instrument to promote food security by ensuring higher food (cereals) consumption levels.

SUMMARY

A substantial amount of empirical work was done in India on food production, food security, distributional aspects and welfare measures which aim at improving the nutritional status of the people. In the existing literature large amount of effort could be observed on nutritional indicators as per capita income or expenditure and on the extent of inequality and poverty. But, not much work was done on intake of nutrition. Large number of studies focused on the average intake of calorie and protein and the size distribution of such intake across the population in different states. Inter-state inequality in intake of nutrients was estimated with the use of available secondary data. Large volumes of literature based on the field survey or primary data are available on nutritional status conducted by nutritional experts in the medical, anthropological, nutritional experts, are available. But basically these studies take into consideration the only anthropometric data to analyse the nutritional status and mal-nutrition of the persons. Generally, these studies were carried out for specific groups of population like children, women and for specific regions like tribal population. The studies which assess the influence of the agricultural development on nutritional status of household are scanty. Particularly, the studies based on the primary data are meager. Thus any study which aims at understanding the influence of agricultural development on the nutritional status of the rural people gains importance due to first hand information on household level.

FOOTNOTES

1. P.G.K. Panikar (1980): "Inter-Regional Variations in Calorie Intake", Economic and Political Weekly, Vol XV, No. 41, 42 & 43, pp. 1803-1814.
2. Rajaram Dasgupta (1983): "Estimation of Nutritional intakes", *Economical and Political Weekly*, Vol. XVIII, No.28, July 9, pp.1288 – 1245.
3. Rajaram Dasgupta (1984): Nutritional Situation of India: A statistical Analysis, Economic and Political Weekly, Vol. XIX, No.34, August, 25.
4. C Gopalan (1995): Towards food and Nutrition Security, Economic and Political Weekly, Vol. XXX, No. 52, December 30, pp. A-134 to A-141.
5. J V Meenakshi, Brinda Vishwanathan (2003): Calorie Deprivation in rural India, 1983-1999/2000, *Economic and Political Weekly*, Vol. XXXVIII, No. 4, January 25, pp.369375.
6. Ramachandran, Prema (2004): The Nutrition Scene in India: Time Trends. NFI Bulletin, Vol. 25(2), pp. 1-5.
7. Ramesh Golait and N. C. Pradhan (2006): Changing Food Consumption Pattern in Rural India: Implication of that on Food and Nutrition security, *Indian Journal of Agricultural Economics*, Vol. 61, No. 3, July-Sept, pp. 374-388.
8. Praduman Kumar, Mruthyunjaya and Madan M Dev (2007): Long-term Changes in Indian Food Basket and Nutrition, *Economic and Political Weekly*, September 1, pp. 3567–3572.
9. Ranjan Ray (2007): Dietary Changes, Calorie Intake and Under-nourishment: A Comparative Study of India and Vietnam, International Seminar on "Revisiting the Poverty Issue: Measurement, Identification and Eradication" in Patna, India, July 20-22. and Discussion Paper 2007-01, School of Economics & Finance, University of Tasmania, Australia.
10. Amartya Sen, Sunil Sengupta (1983): Mal nutrition of Rural children and the Sex Bias, Economic and Political Weekly, Vol. XVIII, No.19, 20 & 21.
11. Cowan, B., and J. Dhanoa. (1983): The prevention of toddler malnutrition by home-based nutrition health education, In Nutrition in the community: A critical look at nutrition policy, planning, and programs, ed. D. S. Mclaren, 339-356. New York: John Wiley and Sons.
12. Pettigrew, J. (1986): Child neglect in rural Punjabi families, *Journal of Comparative Family Studies*, Vol. 17, No. 1, pp.63-85.
13. Behrman, J. 1988a. Nutrition, health birth order, and seasonality: Intrahousehold allocation among children in rural India. Journal of Development Economics, Vol.28, No. 1, pp. 43-62. Behrman, J. 1988b.

Intrahousehold allocation of nutrients in rural India: Are boys favored? Do parents exhibit inequality? *Oxford Economic Papers*, Vol.40, No.1, pp. 32-54.

Behrman, J. R., and A. B. Deolalikar (1990): The intrahousehold demand for nutrients in rural South India. *Journal of Human Resources*, Vol.25, No.4, pp. 665-696.

14. D. Hanumantha Rao, G.N.V. Brahman, K. Mallikharjuna Rao, Ch. Gal Reddy, and N. Pralhad Rao (1993): Assessment of Nutritional Status of 'Jenu Kurubas' – A Primitive Tribe of Karnataka, *The Indian Journal of Nutrition and Diet.*, No. 30, pp. 66-71.
15. Santosh Sangwan, Sudha Chhikara and Shakuntala Punia (1993): Factors Affecting Nutritional Status, *The Indian Journal of Nutrition and Diet.*, No. 30, pp. 159-166.
16. I.V. Parthasarathy and K. Sheela (1993): Effect of Public Distribution System of Foodgrains on Consumption and Nutritional Status of Selected Children, *The Indian Journal of Nutrition and Diet.*, No. 30, pp. 253 -258.
17. Dalip Kumar and T.M. Dak (1993): Food Security in Haryana: A Longitudinal survey, *The Indian Journal of Nutrition and Diet.*, No. 30, pp. 14-18.
18. Ruby Sain (1994): "Nutritional Status of Tribal Children in Birbhum District", *Economical Political Weekly*, Vol. XXIX, No.25, June 18, p.1513.
19. Bombale S.M., Thakare R.P., Borude S.G., and Torane, S.R. (1995): "Nutritional Status of the Agricultural Labour in Thane District (M.S.)", *The Indian Journal of Nutrition and Diet.*, No. 32, pp. 73-78.
20. Jayalakshmi N. and Neelakantan S (1995): "Effect of Socio-economic Status on the Consumption of Food Items and Nutrients", *The Indian Journal of Nutrition and Diet.*, No. 32, pp. 194-197.
21. S.Geetha (1996): "Nutritional Status of Slum Children of Mumbai- A socioeconomic survey", *Economical Political Weekly*, vol.XXXI No.14, April 6, pp.896–900.
22. A.K. Rajula Devi (2001): Food Poverty and Consumption among Landless Labour Households, *Economic and Political Weekly*, XXXVI, No. 28, July 14, pp. 2656-2664.
23. N. Arlappa, N. Balakrishna, Sharad Kumar, G. N. V. Brahmam, K. Vijayaraghavan (2003): "Diet and Nutritional Status of the Elderly in Rural India", *Journal of Nutrition for the Elderly*, Vol. 22, Issue 4, pp 35-52.
24. ACC/SCN (2004) : Fifth Report on the World Nutrition Situation ; Nutrition for Improved Development Outcomes, United Nations Administrative Committee on Co-ordination standing Committee on Nutrition, Geneva.
25. Manu, N. Khetarpaul (2006): "Food consumption pattern of Indian rural preschool children (four to five years)", *British Food Journal*, Vol. 108, Issue 2, pp.127–140.
26. Veera Kumari and R.K.P. Singh (2006): Food Security in Rural Bihar: A Village Level Survey, *Journal of Rural development*, Vol. 25, No. 4, pp. 579-594, NIRD, Hyderabad.

27. Dr. Kaushik Bose, Dilip Bhunia, Ganesh Paul, Ashish Mukhopadhyay and Raja Chakraborty (2006): Age and Sex Variations in Undernutrition of Rural Bengalee Primary School Children of East Midnapore District, West Bengal, India, Human Ecology Special Issue No. 14, pp. 71-75
28. Maithili Ramachandran, K.S. Kavi Kumar and Brinda Viswanathan (2006): Vulnerability to Chronic Energy Deficiency: An Empirical Analysis of Women in Uttar Pradesh, India, WORKING PAPER 12/2006, Madras School of Economics, Gandhi Mandapam Road, Chennai, India.
29. Pushpamma P, Geervani P, Rani MU (1982): Food Intake and Nutrient Adequacy of Rural Population in Andhra Pradesh- India, Human Nutrition, Applied Nutrition, Vol. 36A , No.(4), pp.293-301
30. Jere R. Behrman, Anil B. Deolalikar (1990): The Intrahousehold Demand for Nutrients in Rural South India: Individual Estimates, Fixed Effects, and Permanent Income, *The Journal of Human Resources*, Vol. 25, No. 4, pp. 665-696
31. Kupputhai U. and Mallika N. (1993): Nutritional status of Adult Women belonging to Khond, Gadaba and Porja Tribes of Andhra Pradesh, *The Indian Journal of Nutrition and Diet*, No. 30, pp. 173-179.
32. B. Shantha Kumari and B. Sarada (1993): Food and Nutrient Intake of Vegetable Grower Farmer's Families, *The Indian Journal of Nutrition and Diet.t*, No. 30, pp. 332-339.
33. P. Yasoda Devi and P. Geervani (1994): Determinants of nutrition status of rural preschool children in Andhra Pradesh, India, *Food and Nutrition Bulletin*, Volume 15 (1993/1994), Number 4, December 1994.
34. P.Y.B. Reddy and A. Papa Rao (1995) Protein and Calorie adequacy Status among the Sugals–A Tribal Population of Andhra Pradesh, *The Indian Journal of Nutrition and Diet*, No. 32, pp. 60-64.
35. Prameela Y., Chittemma Rao K. and Sarojini G (1995): A comparative Study on the Nutritional Status of the Rural Adolescent girls Boys (11-18) in Andhra Pradesh, *The Indian Journal of Nutrition and Diete.t*, No. 32, pp. 175-179.
36. Khader V. (1996): Food intake and nutrient adequacy of rural population of Guntur district of Andhra Pradesh, *Indian Journal of Medical Sciences*, Vol. 50, No. 2, pp. 34-42.
37. Schmid M. A., Egeland G. M., Salomeyesudas B., Satheesh P. V., Kuhnlein H. V. (2001): "Traditional food consumption and nutritional status of Dalit mothers in rural Andhra Pradesh, South India", Deccan Development Society, Hyderabad.
38. B. Sambi Reddy (2004): Food Security in regional Perspective: The Case of Andhra Pradesh, Journal of Rural Development, Vol. 23(3), pp. 319-333.

3

SOCIO-ECONOMIC PROFILE OF THE STUDY AREA AND SAMPLE HOUSEHOLDS

This Chapter has been divided into two sections. Section–I presents the profile of the selected districts and villages. The geographical area, location, population, number of mandals and villages in the district, workers, facilities and infrastructure etc. and other aspects of the districts as well as villages are presented in this section. Section–II presents the socio-economic profile of the sample households. The profile relates to size of the household, caste, literacy, landholding, age of the head of household, occupation etc. and other aspects of households in both canal irrigated and rain-fed villages.

SECTION – I

Information on the total area and its administrative divisions, population characteristics, agriculture and climatic conditions, crops grown and live stock population etc., of the two Costal District of Andhra Pradesh viz., East Godavari and Vizianagaram Districts was presented in this Section. Along with the district profile, the details of the selected villages namely Repuru and Gutchimi of East Godavari and Vizianagaram districts respectively also are presented in this Section.

PROFILE OF CANAL IRRIGATED DISTRICT–EAST GODAVARI AND THE SELECTED VILLAGE REPURU

Geographical and Physical Location

East Godavari District is located on the North – East of Andhra Pradesh in the geographical co-ordinats of 16^0 – 30^0 and 18^0 – 20^0 of the Northern Longitude and 18^0 -30^0 and 82^0 – 36^0 of Eastern Latitude. East Godavari District can be broadly classified into three natural divisions namely the Delta, Upland and Agency or hill tracts. The general elevation of the district varies from a few meters near the sea to about 300 meters in the hills of the agency. The Eastern Ghats rise by gradations from the level of the coast and spread throughout the erstwhile agency Taluks of Rampachodavaram and Yellavaram. The delta portion constituting the whole of Konaseema and

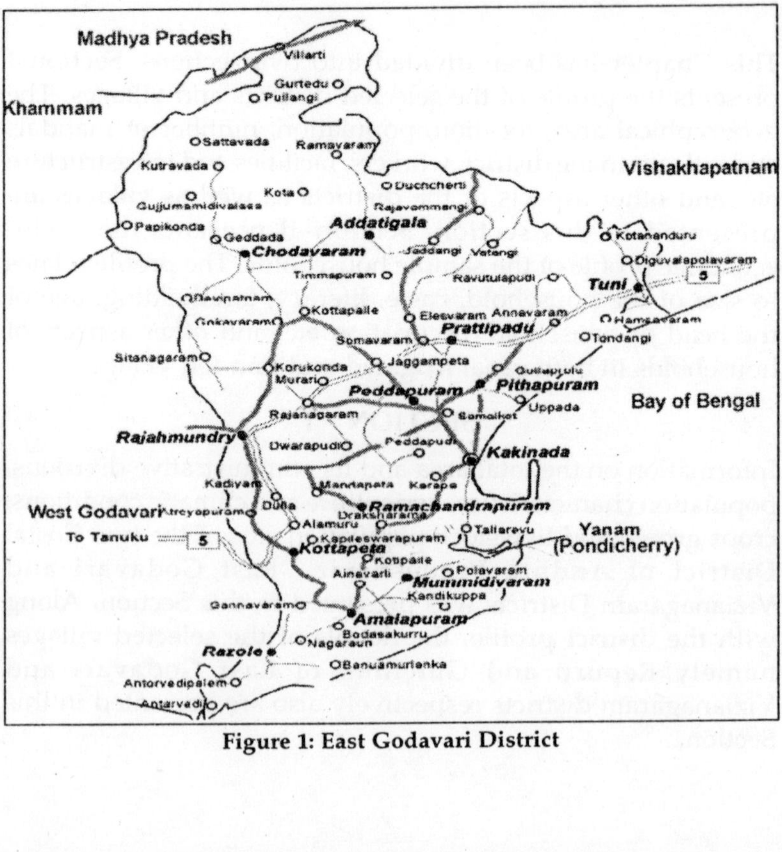

Figure 1: East Godavari District

portions of Kakinada, Ramachandrapuram and Rajahmundry erstwhile Taluks, presents a vast expanse of rice-fields surrounded by plantain, betel, coconut gardens and innumerable palmyrah trees. The erstwhile Taluks of Tuni, Pithapuram, Peddapuram and portions of Kakinada, Ramachandrapuram and Rajahmundry constitute the upland areas. The main soils in the District are alluvial (clay loamy) red soil, sandy loam and sandy clay. There is mostly alluvial soil in Godavari delta and sandy clay soil at the tail end portions of the Godavari River, red loamy soil in upland and agency area. The total geographical area of the District is 10,807 sq km.

Land Utilisation

About 45 percent of the total area of the district is cultivable and 50 percent of cultivable area is irrigated. Table 1 presents the details of the land utilization in the district. It could be observed from the Table that the total area covered by forests forms 29.86 percent.Net area sown has been increasing over the period of time.

Table 1
Land Utilisation 2002-05 in Canal Irrigated District

(Hectares)

	Years		
Category	*2002-03*	*2003-04*	*2004-05*
Forest	323107	323107	323107
Barren and Cultivable Land	82716	8234	82282
Land put to non-agricultural Use	123530	131945	132070
Cultivable Waste	16490	16441	6415
Permanent pastures and other grazing lands	24822	23643	23541
Land under miscellaneous tree crops and grooves not included in net area sown	8112	8208	8209
Current fallows	70029	1215	17502
Other fallow lands	23435	66367	60220
Net area sown	409602	428587	418496
Total Geographical area	1081842	1081842	1081842
Total Cropped Area	368057	764139	735450
Area sown more than once	238742	328912	311499

Source: Chief Planning Officer, East Godavari District, 2005-06

The District is divided into Five Revenue Divisions comprising of 60 mandals. Out of that 58 are rural mandals and only two are urban mandals. There are 1,379 villages in the District.

Table 2
Administrative Divisions of the East Godavari District

No. of Revenue Disivions	5
No. of Erstwhile Taluks	19
No. of Revenue Mandals	60 (58 Rural + 2 Urban)
No. of Mandal Praja Parishads	57
No. of Gram Panchayats	1011
No. of Municipalities	7
No. of Municipal Corporations	2
No. of Villages	1379

Source: Chief Planning Officer, East Godavari District, 2005-06

Demographic Characteristics

Population

According to the 2001 census the total population of the District was 48,72,622 at which 50.20 percent are males and 49.80 percent are females. It could be observed that female population is higher than male population in urban areas. The sex ratio is low in rural areas.

Table 3
Population Composition in Rural and Urban Areas–2001 Census

	Total	*Male*	*Female*	*Sex Ratio*
Rural	3735908 (76.67)	1877779 (38.54)	1858129 (38.13)	990
Urban	1136714 (23.33)	568032 (11.66)	568682 (11.67)	1001
Total	4872622 (100.00)	2445811 (50.20)	2426811 (49.80)	992

Source: Chief Planning Officer, East Godavari District, 2005-06

Literacy

The literacy rate in the district is 65.49 percent and the rural literacy rates are lower than urban literacy rate.

Table 4
The Levels of Literacy in East Godavari District

	Total	*Male*	*Female*	*Literacy Rate*
Rural	2050482	1100881	949601	62.52
Urban	762636	406107	356529	75.11
Total	2813118	1506988	130613	65.49

Source: Chief Planning Officer, East Godavari District, 2005-06

Occupation

The primary occupation of the population of the district is agriculture. It could be observed from Table 5 that the proportion of cultivators in the district is higher than that of agricultural labour. It could also be observed that the proportion of non-workers is higher than that of workers.

Table 5
Occupational Pattern of the Workers 2001 of East Godavari District

Occupation of Workers	*No of Persons (lakhs)*	*Percentage to Total Population*
Cultivators	21.9	44.69
Agricultural Labourers	9.86	20.12
Main Workers	16.13	32.91
Marginal Workers	3.15	6.42
Non-workers	29.61	60.42
Total Population	49.04	100.00

Source: Chief Planning Officer, East Godavari District, 2005-06

Area Under Various Crops

Table 6 furnishes particulars of the irrigated area under principal crops in East Godavari District during 2000-05. It could be observed that area under paddy is decreasing during this period from 3,97,036 hectares to 3,77,321 hectares. In case of chillies, ground nuts, tobacco the same trend of decline could be observed. Area under sesamum remained almost constant but area under sugarcane recorded an increase from 21,476 hectares in 2000-01 to 26,562 in 2004-05.

Table 6
Area Under Various Crops during 2004-05

(Hectares)

Crops	*2000-01*	*2001-02*	*2002-03*	*2003-04*	*2004-05*
Paddy	3,97,036	3,76,835	2,95,287	3,87,492	3,77,321
Sugarcane	21,476	20,835	24,596	25,242	26,562
Chillies	530	894	503	1,151	242
Ground Nuts	250	114	194	239	158
Sesamum	387	334	490	514	397
Tobacco	1,956	1,699	1,681	1,801	1,046

Source: Chief Planning Officer, Kakinada, East Godavari District, 2005-06

Climate and Rain Fall

The climate is comparatively moderate throughout the year except during the months of April to June when the temperature reaches a maximum of 48 deg. centigrade. The normal rainfall of the District is 1280.0 mm. More than half of the rainfall is brought by South-West Monsoon while the rest from the North-East Monsoon, during October and November.

Agriculture and Crops

East Godavari District is situated in Krishna Godavari Agro Climatic Zone. It is one of the agriculturally potential districts in Andhra Pradesh, contributing about 10% of the total food production of the State. It is broadly classified into four Agro Climatic Zones:

1. Central delta,
2. Eastern Delta,
3. Upland area and
4. Agency area.

Paddy

The major crop grown in the District is paddy which is cultivated both in Kharif and Rabi seasons as Irrigated and Unirrigated crop. During Kharif 2001 an area of 2.10 lakh ha of area is cultivated as irrigated paddy and production is 8.42

lakh tonnes with productivity of 3994 Kg/ha (paddy). Further, in an area of 9930 ha paddy is grown as unirrigated crop with a production of 0.17 lakh tonnes and productivity of 1716 Kg/ha. During Rabi 2001-02 paddy is grown in an area of 1.66 Lakh ha and the production is 10.97 lakh tonnes with a productivity of 3625 Kg/ha.

Maize

Maize crop grown both in Kharif and Rabi. In Kharif 2001 the crop was grown in an area of 2495 ha with a production of 6442 tonnes and productivity is 2582 Kg/ha. In Rabi 2001-02 an area of 3241 ha is covered with Maize and production is 10770 tonnes with productivity of 3323 Kg/ha.

Jowar

During Kharif 2001, Jowar crop is grown in 999 ha of area and the production is 1094 Tonnes with productivity of 1095 Kg/ha.

Pulses

Black gram and green gram is the major crops grown under pulses in both Kharif and Rabi. An area of 15931 ha is covered with black gram in the year 2001 with a production of 5958 tonnes and the productivity is 374 Kg/ha.

Oil Seeds

Under oil seeds major crops grown here are esamum and ground nut in both Kharif & Rabi. In Kharif 2001 an area of 2843 ha is covered under esamum and the production is 640 tonnes and productivity is 225 Kg/ha. In Rabi 2001-02, 1629 ha of area is covered with esamum and the production and productivity are 459 tonnes and 282 Kg/ha respectively.

Sugar Cane

During 2001 sugarcane was grown in 15778 ha and the production and productivity are 1410 lakh tonnes and 8940 tonnes/ha respectively.

Animal Husbandry

The live stock and poultry population in East Godavari District as per Livestock Census of 1999 is about 11.77 lakhs. Total cattle stock account for about 3.36 lakhs. Total buffaloes are about 4.98 lakh, sheep, goats and pigs are about 66 thousand, 1.55 lakhs and 47 thousand respectively. Total poultry birds are about 76 lakhs.

Table 7
Live Stock Population of the East Godavari District, 1991

Animal	*Numbers*
Cattle	3,36,073
Buffaloes	4,98,448
Sheep	66,599
Pigs	47,464
Goat	1,55,100
Dog	74,138
Horses & Ponies	272
Total Live Stock	11,77,832
Total Poultry	76,50,996

Source: http://www.aponline.gov.in/

Table 8
Salient features of Canal irrigated Village–Repuru (1991)

Item	*Description*
Total area of the Village (ha.)	263.85
Irrigated (ha.)	150.54
Source of Irrigation (ha.)	Government Canal
Unirrigated (ha.)	12.14
Culturable Waste (ha.)	9.31
Area not available for cultivation (ha.)	91.86

Source: Census 1991, District Profiles, Village Directory.

Table 8 presents the details of the Repuru Village of Kakinada Rural Mandal according to 1991 census. The total geographical area of the village is 263.85 hectares. Out of which 171.99 hectares is used for cultivation. 87.05 percent is irrigated and 7.06 percent is unirrigated. The village survey was conducted during January 2007. In the village there are 817 households. The following Tables-9, 10 and 11 present the occupational, caste, and literacy details of the households.

Table 9
Occupational Structure of the Households, Repuru Village

Occupation	*No. of Households*
Cultivators	168
Agricultural labour	402
Non- agricultural Workers	126
Business	39
Service	31
Employees	51
Total	817

Table 10
Literacy Level of the Heads of the Household, Repuru Village

Education Level	*No. of Househols*
Illiterate	392
Primary	290
Secondary	119
Above secondary	16
Total	817

Table 11
Caste of the Households, Repuru Village

Caste	*No. of Households*
Padmasali	2
Brahmin	10
Setti Balija	43
Kapu	675
Dudekula Saheb	43
Chowdary	1
Reddika	1
Relli	1
Rajaka	31
Schedule Tribe	2
Schedule Caste	8
Total	817

PROFILE OF RAIN-FED DISTRICT–VIZIANAGARAM AND SELECTED VILLAGE-GUTCHIMI

Vizianagaram District is one of the northern coastal districts of AndhraPradesh. Vizianagaram city is the district head quarter. This District was formed on 1 June 1979, with some parts carved from the neighbouring districts of Vishakhapatnam and Srikakulam. In Telugu Vizia means Victory and Nagaram means city. The district was named after the princely state of Vizianagaram.

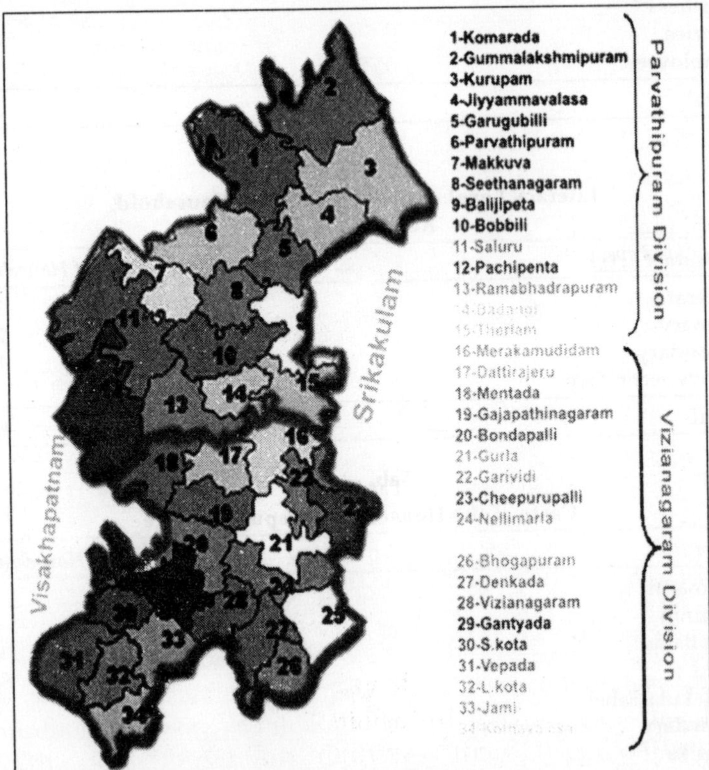

Figure 2: Vizianagaram District

Geographical and Physical Location

Vizianagaram district is situated in the geographical area of 17°-15′and 19°-15′ of the Northern latitude and 83°-00′and 83°-

45′ of the Eastern longitude. Vizianagaram is bounded in east by Srikakulum district. Southern and western parts are bounded by Vishakhapatnam. Bay of Bengal is in the southeast part and northwest is bounded by Orissa. The District can be divided into two distinct natural divisions.i.e, plains and hilly areas. The hilly area covers Pachipenta and Gummalaxmipuram mandals and Salur, Makkuva, Ramabhadrapuram, Pavarthipuram and Komarada mandals. The rest are plains. The average height of the hills is 914 meters, although there are several peaks of 1,219 meters high. The total area of the district is 6,30,038 hectors.

Land Utilisation

Table 12 presents the details of the land utilization in the district. It may be observed that about 51.1% of the land area is used for agriculture and another 12.3% land is put under non-agricultural uses, 17.8% covered by forests and 12.3% of the land is Barren and uncultivable. Net area sown is 49 percent of the total geographical area.

Table 12
Land Utilisation 2001 in Vizianagaram District

(Hectares)

Category	*2001*	*% to Gross Area*
Forest	111977	17.8
Barren and Cultivable Land	77753	12.3
Land put to non-agricultural Use	76172	12.1
Current fallows	24232	3.9
Other fallow lands	31145	4.9
Net area sown	308759	49.0
Total Geographical area	630038	100.0

Source: Census 2001

The district is divided into two revenue divisions comprising 34 mandals. There are in total 1,551 villages. Details are presented in Table 13.

Table 13
Administrative Divisions of Vizianagaram District

No. of Revenue Disivions	2
No. of Revenue Mandals	34
No. of Gram Panchayats	931
No. of Municipalities	4
No. of Villages	1551

Source: Census, 2001.

Demographic Characteristics

Population

Table 14 presents the details of the population of Vizianagaram district. According to 2001 census the total population of the district was 21,10,943 at which 50 percent are male population and 50 percent are female population. Sex ratio is 1000.

Table 14
Population Composition in Rural and Urban Areas–2001 Census

	Total	*Male*	*Female*	*Sex Ratio*
Rural	1747443 (82.78)	874195 (41.41)	873248 (41.37)	1000
Urban	363500 (17.22)	181140 (8.58)	182360 (8.64)	1010
Total	2110943 (100.00)	1055335 (50.00)	1055608 (50.00)	1000

Source: Census, 2001

Literacy

The literacy rate in the district is 51.07 percent and the female literacy rate is lower than male literacy rate (Table 15) .

Table 15
The Literacy Level in Vizianagaram District

Gender	*Literacy Rate*
Male	62.37
Female	39.91
Total	51.07

Source: Census, 2001

Occupation

Primary occupation of the population is agriculture. It could be observed from Table 12 that the difference between proportion of cultivators and agricultural labourers is marginal, and the proportion of workers and non-workers is also equal in the district (Table 16).

Table 16
Occupational Pattern of Workers, 2001 Census–Vizianagaram District

Occupation of the Workers	*No of Persons (lakhs)*	*Percentage to Total Population*
Cultivators	8.10	38.38
Agricultural Labour	7.22	34.19
Main Workers	9.60	45.49
Marginal Workers	1.02	4.84
Non-workers	10.49	49.67
Total Population	21.11	100.00

Source: Chief Planning Officer, Vizianagaram District, 2005-06

Climate and Railfall

The climate of district is hot and humidity level is very high with good rainfall through out the year. Normal rainfall of the district for the year is 1,131.0 mm.

Agriculture

Vizianagaram is prominently an agricultural district as 68.4% of the workers are engaged in agriculture. 82% of the population lives in rural areas and depends on agriculture. 80% of the cultivation is done under rain fed conditions. Even the irrigated area also depends on the rainfall. Hence the majority of the crops grown are dry crops. Paddy crop is cultivated mainly during Kharif season with 80% of the area under tanks, which in turn depends on rainfall. Major crops are Paddy, Mesta, Groundnut, Ragi, Bajra, Cotton, Sugarcane and Pulses. Principal rivers are Nagavali, Suvarnamukhi, Vegavati, Champavati, Gosthani and Kandivalasa. There are no major irrigation projects in the district. Only 12 medium irrigation projects are functioning with 43,984 hecters of land and other minor 1,065 irrigation sources have 51,215 hecters, and 8,616 minor irrigation tanks with 72,112 hecters of area under irrigation.

Live Stock

Table 17 presents the details of the live stock population of the Vizianagaram district.

Table 17
Live Stock Population of the Vizianagaram District

Animal	*Numbers (in Lakhs)*
Cattle	4.00
Buffaloes	2.50
Sheep	5.13
Pigs	0.31
Goat	1.97
Total Live Stock	13.91
Total Poultry	21.30

Source: http://www.aponline.gov.in/

The live stock in Vizianagaram district as per the 2004 census is about 13.91 lakhs. Cattle stock account for about 4 lakhs. Buffaloes are about 2.5 lakh. Sheep, goats and pigs are about 5.13 lakhs, 1.97 lakhs and 31 thousand respectively. Poultry birds are about 21.30 lakhs.

Table 18
The Salient Feature of Rain-fed Village-Gutchimi (1991)(ha.)

Item	*Description*
Total area of the Village	596.51
Forest	62
Irrigated	183.00
Source of Irrigation	Tank
Unirrigated	304.54
Culturable Waste	35
Area not available for cultivation	12

Source: Census 1991, District Profiles, Village Directory.

Table 18 presents the details of the Gutchimi Village of Seethanagaram Mandal according to 1991 census. Total geographical area of the village is 596.51 hectares. Out of which 12 hectares is not available for cultivation. 183 hectares is irrigated and 304.54 hectares is unirrigated. Village survey was conducted during January 2007. In the village there are 493 households. Tables 19, 20 and 21 present the occupational, caste, and literacy details of the households.

Table 19
Occupational Structure of the Households of Gutchimi Village

Occupation	*No. of Households*
Cultivators	210
Agricultural labourers	32
Non- agricultural Workers	124
Business	52
Service	23
Employees	52
Total	493

Table 20
Literacy Level of the Heads of the Household of Gutchimi Village

Occupation	*No. of Households*
Illiterate	276
Primary	96
Secondary	102
Above secondary	19
Total	493

Table 21
Caste of the Households of Gutchimi Village

Caste	*No. of Households*
Koppala Velama	317
Viswa Brahmin	25
Padmasali	19
Nai Brahmin	4
Vaisya	17
Sista Karanam	4
Jangalu	81
Jalari	6

Contd.

Caste	*No. of Households*
Schedule Tribe	6
Schedule Caste	2
Brahmin	1
Kummari	2
Rajaka	9
Total	493

SECTION – II

PROFILE OF THE SELECTED SAMPLE HOUSEHOLDS

In this Section an attempt is made to study the social aspects like caste, family size, age and literacy of the head of the household, and some economic aspects like occupation, land ownership, cattle etc., of the sample households.

Religion

The details of the religion of the sample households are presented in Table 22. It may be seen that majority of the sample households in rain-fed village belongs to Hindu religion compared to canal irrigated village..

Table 22
Distribution of Households According to Religion

Type of Village	*Hindu*	*Christian*	*Total*
Canal Irrigated	179	25	204
	(87.7)	(12.3)	(100.00)
Rain-fed	120	4	124
	(96.8)	(3.2)	(100.00)

Caste

Caste is one of the characteristics of the households that specify the social position of the households in the society and to some extent influence the family income. The details of the distribution of the sample households by caste are given in Table 23. It could be seen that in the canal irrigated village Kapu is the dominated caste where 71.6 percent of the sample households belongs to this caste. Where as in the rain-fed village Koppula Velama is the dominant caste where 66.1 percent of the sample households belongs to this caste.

Table 23
Distribution of Households According to Caste

Type of Village	*Kapu*	*Koppula velama*	*Vishwa Brahmin*	*Rajak*	*Madiga*	*Mala*	*Others*	*Total*
Canal Irrigated	146 (71.6)	-	3 (1.5)	21 (10.3)	6 (2.9)	25 (12.3)	3 (1.5)	204 (100.00)
Rain-fed	-	82 (66.1)	9 (7.3)	8 (6.5)	3 (2.4)		22 (17.7)	124 (100.00)

Gender of the Head of the Household

In recent years the phenomenon of female headed households is gradually increasing all over world. Table 24 presents the distribution of the households according to the gender. It could be observed that among the sample households in the rain-fed village the percentage of female headed households is more than canal irrigated village.

Table 24
Distribution of Households According to Gender of the Head of the Household

Type of Village	*Male*	*Female*	*Total*
Canal Irrigated	194 (95.1)	10 (4.9)	204 (100.00)
Rain-fed	110 (88.7)	14 (11.3)	124 (100.00)

Age of the Head of the Household

The age of the head of the household may influence his productive capacity and the composition of the family. The distribution of the households according to the age of the head of the households is presented in Table 25. They are grouped under five categories. It could be observed that the percentage of sample households having heads below the age of 36 years is higher in canal irrigated village compared to rain-fed village where as the percentage of sample households having above the age of 65 years is higher in rain-fed village than canal irrigated village. The one common feature is that majority of the sample households are between the age of 36 and 55 years.

Table 25
Distribution of Head of the Households According to Age Group

Type of Village	*<=35*	*36 – 45*	*46 – 55*	*56 – 65*	*>= 66*	*Total*
Canal Irrigated	53	65	53	24	9	204
	(26.0)	(31.8)	(26.0)	(11.8)	(4.4)	(100.00)
Rain-fed	8	41	46	20	9	124
	(6.5)	(33.0)	(37.1)	(16.1)	(7.3)	(100.00)

Literacy

The role of literacy in human development is well recognized. The literacy levels of the head of the households are presented in Table 26. The percentage of households headed by illiterates is more in canal irrigated village than rain-fed village. In similar manner percentage of households heads having secondary level or above education is also more in canal irrigated village than rain-fed village.

Table 26
Literacy Level of the Head of the Households

Type of Village	*Illiterate*	*Primary*	*Secondary*	*Above Secondary*	*Total*
Canal Irrigated	97	41	46	20	204
	(47.5)	(20.1)	(22.5)	(9.8)	(100.00)
Rain-fed	51	36	30	7	124
	(41.4)	(29.0)	(24.2)	(5.6)	(100.00)

Family Size

Distribution of the sample households according to family size is presented in Table 27. The households are categorized to three groups. It could be seen that almost equal proportion of households in both the villages belongs to the group of 1-3 member households. In case of rain-fed village households, more proportion of households are having big family size compared to canal irrigated village.

Table 27
Distribution of Households According to Family Size

Type of Village	*1-3*	*4-6*	*7 and above*	*Total*
Canal Irrigated	40	156	8	204
	(19.6)	(76.4)	(4.0)	(100.00)
Rain-fed	24	88	12	124
	(19.4)	(70.9)	(9.7)	(100.00)

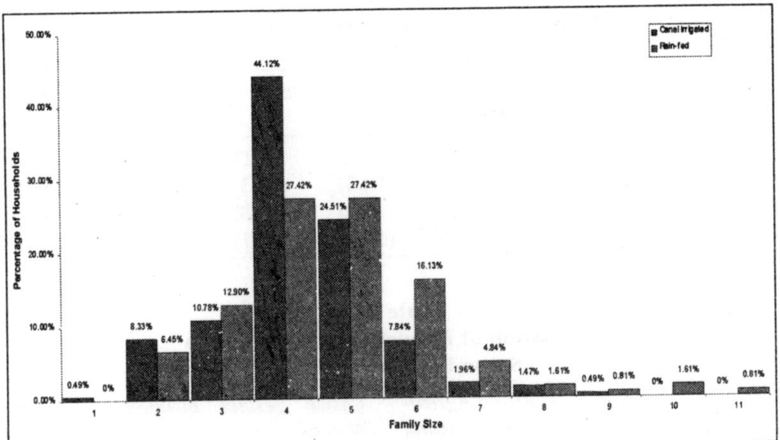

Figure 3: Distribution of Households by Size of Family

The distributions of household size for canal irrigated and rain-fed villages are presented graphically in Figure 3. It reveals that households with 4 or 5 members accounted for around 68% in canal irrigated village where as they account for 55% in rain-fed village.

Occupation of the Head of the Household

Occupational status of the head of the households effects the food consumption and nutritional status. Good occupation resulting in higher demand for food and will in turn result more nutritional status.

Table 28 presents the distribution of the households according to the main occupation. In the canal irrigated village highest percentage of heads of the sample households is agricultural labourers (34.3 percent) followed by cultivators (29.9 percent). Where as in the rain-fed village highest percentage is cultivators (32.3 percent) followed by agricultural labours (20.2 percent). Almost equal share could be observed with respect to occupations of service, business and employment in both the villages.

Table 28
Distribution of Households According to Main Occupation

Type of Village	*Cultivator*	*Agricultural Labour*	*Services*	*Business*	*Employed*	*Total*
Canal Irrigated	61 (29.9)	79 (38.7)	21 (10.3)	21 (10.3)	22 (10.8)	204 (100.00)
Rain-fed	40 (32.3)	25 (20.2)	20 (16.1)	20 (16.1)	19 (15.1)	124 (100.00)

Table 29
Distribution of Households According to Secondary Occupation

Type of Village	*No Secondury Occupation*	*Cultivator*	*Agricultural Labour*	*Casual Worker*	*Service*	*Business*	*Total*
Canal Irrigated	180 (88.2)	12 (5.3)	10 (4.9)	1 (0.5)	1 (0.5)	-	204 (100.00)
Rain-fed	67 (54.00)	23 (18.5)	-	27 (21.80	-	7 (5.60	124 (100.00)

Table 29 presents the distribution of households according to secondary occupation in canal irrigated village majority of the households are not pursuing any secondary occupation (88.2 percent) signifies the adequacy of the work in the main occupation itself through out the year. Generally there will be no slack season which will effect the earning and opportunities for getting work in this village. In case of rain-fed village nearly half of the heads of the household are pursuing secondary occupation in order to feed their families. It clearly indicates the failure of agricultural sector in providing year long employment to the sample households in rain-fed village. No household is having secondary occupation as agricultural labour. Cultivation is only secondary occupation for nearly 18 percent of sample households in rain-fed village. Highest percent of households are depending on casual work as secondary occupation.

Size of Land Holding

The distribution of the sample households by size of wet land possessed in both the canal irrigated and rain-fed villages are presented in Table 30. It can be noted that in canal irrigated village only 37.7 percent of the households possess wet land and in that a majority of the sample households (28.9 percent) possess less than or equal to 3 acres. Where as in rain-fed village around 67.7 percent of the sample households possess wet land and majority of the households (42.7 percent) belong to less than or equal to 3 acres.

Table 30
Distribution of Households According to Wet Land Possessed

(Acres)

Type of Village	*No Land*	*<=3*	*3 <=6*	*> 6*	*Total*
Canal Irrigated	127	59	14	4	204
	(62.3)	(28.9)	(6.8)	(2.00)	(100.00)
Rain-fed	40	53	22	9	124
	(32.3)	(42.7)	(17.7)	(7.3)	(100.00)

The distribution of the sample households by size of dry land possessed in both the canal irrigated and rain-fed villages are presented in Table 31. It can be noted that in canal irrigated village only less than 10 percent of the households possess dry land and in that a majority of the sample households (8.3 percent) possess less than or equal to 3 acres. This clearly indicated the improved irrigation facilities in the East Godavari district. Where as in rain-fed village more than 30 percent of the sample households possess dry land and even there exist households having more than 6 acres of dry land. Therefore this reveals the dependency of the sample households on rain-fed agriculture in this village.

The common feature in both the villages is highest percentage of the households possess less than 3 acres and villages are dominated by small and marginal farmers.

Table 31
Distribution of Households According to Dry Land Possessed

(In Acres)

Type of Village	*No Land*	*<=3*	*3 <=6*	*> 6*	*Total*
Canal Irrigated	185	17	2	-	204
	(90.7)	(8.3)	(1)		(100.00)
Rain-fed	85	29	7	03	124
	(68.5)	(23.5)	(5.6)	(2.4)	(100.00)

Paddy is the principal cereals crop produced in both the villages by the sample households. The other crop produced in canal irrigated village is the Groundnut. Janumu was cultivated by less proportion of the households in canal irrigated village where as it is the prominent crop produced by sample households of the rain-fed village. Cashew and Sugarcane are the other crops produced in the rained village. This information clearly indicates the cropping differences that exist in rain-fed and canal irrigated villages.

Table 32
Distribution of Households According to Principal Cereal Crops

Type of Village	*Paddy*	*Janumu*	*Sugar*	*Cashew*	*Groundnut*
Canal Irrigated	83	4	-	-	22
Rain-fed	88	44	27	88	3

Table 33
Distribution of Households According to Milch Cattle Owned

Type of Village	*Buffalos*	*Cows*	*Total*
Canal Irrigated	51	2	53
Rain-fed	13	11	24

The information on livestock possessed by sample households is presented in Table 33. It could be seen that in rain-fed villages more cows are owned where as in canal irrigated villages more number of buffalos are owned.

Type of the Dwelling House

Type of the dwelling house can be regarded as an indicator for economic status of the household. Table 34 presents the dwelling house particulars of the sample households. It can be observed that more than 55 percent of the sample households in both the canal irrigated and rain-fed villages are residing in tiled houses. In the rain-fed village the proportion of the population residing in R.C.C. slab houses is higher than canal irrigated village. Still some percentage households in rural areas are not having proper dwelling as it is evident from the percentage of households living in thatched houses in both the villages.

Table 34
Distribution of Households According to Type of House

Type of Village	*Thatched*	*Tiled*	*R.C.C.Slab*	*Total*
Canal Irrigated	27	114	63	204
	(13.2)	(55.9)	(30.9)	(100.00)
Rain-fed	6	70	48	124
	(4.8)	(56.5)	(38.7)	(100.00)

Source of Lighting

Table 35 presents the source of lighting of the sample households. Electricity is the source of lighting for the sample households. It could be observed that in the rain-fed village all the households are having electricity.

Table 35
Distribution of Households According to Sources of Energy for Lighting

Type of Village	*Kerosene*	*Electricity*	*Total*
Canal Irrigated	3	201	204
	(1.5)	(98.5)	(100.00)
Rain-fed	-	124	124
		(100.00)	(100.00)

Source of Energy for Cooking

The source of energy for cooking for the sample households is presented in Table 36. Firewood and L.P.G (Liquefied petroleum Gas) are the sources of energy for the sample households.

Table 36
Distribution of Households According to Source of Energy for Cooking

Type of Village	*Kero-sene*	*Fire-wood*	*Gas*	*Firewood + Gas*	*Coal + Gas*	*Coal + firewood*	*Total*
Canal Irrigated	3	116	79	6			204
	(1.5)	(56.9)	(38.7)	(2.3)			(100.00)
Rain-fed	-	67	9	43	2	3	124
		(54)	(7.3)	(37.7)	(1.6)	(2.4)	(100.00)

Source of Drinking Water

Table 37 presents the sources of drinking water in both the villages for sample households. It could be observed that open well and bore well are the major sources of drinking water for the sample households in canal are irrigated village. In case of rain-fed village open well and tap are the major sources of drinking water for the sample households.

Table 37
Distribution of Households According to Source of Drinking Water

Type of Village	*Bore well*	*Open well*	*Open well + tap*	*Open well + Pond*	*Tap + Borewell*	*Tap*	*Canal*	*Total*
Canal	58	102	17	-	17	6	4	204
Irrigated	(28.4)	(50)	(8.4)		(8.3)	(2.9)	(2)	(100.00)
Rain-fed	6	33	59	05	12	9	-	124
	(4.8)	(26.6)	(47.6)	(4.0)	(9.7)	(7.3)		(100.00)

Ration Cards

From Table 38 it is clear that more than 80 percent of the sample households possess 'White Ration Cards'[1]. This means that they are the poor households. Only less than 20 percent of the households are above the poverty line as they possess the Pink Ration Card.

Table 38
Distribution of Households According to Type of Ration Card

Type of Village	*White Colour*	*Pink Colour*	*Total*
Canal Irrigated	164 (80.4)	40 (19.6)	204 (100.00)
Rain-fed	102 (82.3)	22 (17.7)	124 (100.00)

Details of the Household Member

Distribution of the members of household according to the gender is presented in Table 39. The composition of males is higher in canal irrigated village than rain-fed village in the sample households.

Table 39
Gender Composition of the Family Members of the Sample Households

Type of Village	*Male*	*Female*	*Total*
Canal Irrigated	451 (53.12)	398 (46.88)	849 (100.00)
Rain-fed	310 (50.3)	17 (49.7)	616 (100.00)

The distribution of the members of the households according to the age is presented in Table 40. They are grouped under five categories. Majority of the members are below the age of 36 years in both the villages but they are higher in canal irrigated village compared to rain-fed village

Table 40
Age Composition of the Family Members of the Sample Households

Type of Village	*<=35*	*36 – 45*	*46 – 55*	*56 – 65*	*>= 66*	*Total*
Canal Irrigated	562 (66.2)	128 (15.1)	100 (11.8)	44 (5.2)	15 (1.8)	849 (100.00)
Rain-fed	360 (58.4)	112 (18.2)	84 (13.6)	43 (7.0)	17 (2.8)	616 (100.00)

The literacy level of the members of the households is presented in Table 41. Illiterates are more in rain-fed village compared to canal irrigated village. Whereas secondary and above secondary educated are more in rain-fed village than canal irrigated.

Table 41

Literacy Levels of the Family Members of the Sample Households

Type of Village	*Illiterate*	*Primary*	*Secondary*	*Above Secondary*	*Total*
Canal Irrigated	207 (23.8)	254 (29.9)	252 (29.7)	141 (16.6)	849 (100.00)
Rain-fed	214 (34.8)	94 (15.2)	191 (31.0)	107 (18.9)	616 (100.00)

Working status of the members of households is presented in the Table 42. Percentage of non-working population is higher in canal irrigated village compared to the rain-fed village. Cultivators are more in rain-fed village than in canal irrigated village whereas agricultural labourers are more in the canal irrigated than in the rain-fed. This clearly indicates that in the canal irrigated village agriculture is the dominant occupation where most of the people depend on that for their livelihood. In the rain-fed village most of the people depend on casual work for their livelihood and agriculture provides only seasonal employment and generally only farmers engage in that for majority of the days in a year. It could also be observed from the Table that the dependency ratio is 1.41 in canal irrigated village which means per every worker in the household there are 1.5 members who depend on his earnings. Where as in the rain-fed village the dependency ration is only 0.78 means per every worker less than 1 person is dependent on his earnings. It could be expected that when the dependency ratio is low it has a positive impact on the food consumption of the households.

The activity status of the members of households in the last 24 hours for both the genders is presented in the Table 43 and Table 44 for the canal irrigated village and rain-fed village respectively.

There is no significant difference in the usual working status of the members and activity status in the last 24 hours

Table 42

Usual Working Status of the Family Members of the Sample Households

Type of Village	*Non-Workers*	*Cultivators*	*Agricultural Laboures*	*Casual Workers*	*Employees*	*Services*	*Business*	*Dependency Ratio*
Canal Irrigated	498	100	134	13	30	27	47	1.41
	(57.46)	(11.8)	(15.8)	(2.54)	(3.6)	(3.2)	(5.4)	
Rain-fed	270	163	1	65	36	45	36	0.78
	(43.83)	(26.5)	(0.2)	(10.55)	(5.8)	(7.3)	(5.8)	

Table 43
Activity Status of the Family Members of the Sample Households in the last 24 hours in Canal Irrigate Village

Type of Village	*Non-Worker*	*Cultivator*	*Agricultural Labour*	*Casual Worker*	*Employers*	*Services*	*Business*	*Total*
Male	180	84	77	4	25	23	58	451
	(39.9)	(18.6)	(17.1)	(0.9)	(5.6)	(5.1)	(12.9)	(100)
Female	286	17	51	6	3	24	11	398
	(74.9)	(4.3)	(12.8)	(1.5)	(0.8)	(6.0)	(2.8)	(100)
Total	456	101	128	10	28	47	69	849
	(55.00)	(11.9)	(15.1)	(1.2)	(3.3)	(5.5)	(8.1)	(100)

Table 44

Activity Status of the Family Members of the Sample Households in last 24 hours in Rain-Fed Village

Type of Village	*Non-Worker*	*Cultivator*	*Agricultural Labour*	*Casual Worker*	*Employees*	*Services*	*Business*	*Total*
Male	118	88	1	17	27	20	39	310
	(28.1)	(28.4)	(0.3)	(5.5)	(8.7)	(6.5)	(12.6)	(100)
Female	205	73	1	3	6	13	5	306
	(66.9)	(23.9)	(0.3)	(1.0)	(2.0)	(4.2)	(1.6)	(100)
Total	323	161	2	20	33	33	44	616
	(53.0)	(26.1)	(0.3)	(3.2)	(5.3)	(5.4)	(7.1)	(100)

in canal irrigated village. Even though the percentage of people in casual work is slightly low with respect to activity status compared to the working status, activity status is higher than working status with respect to the service and business. The agricultural labour activity is more followed by service activity for the females in canal irrigated, where as cultivation occupies first place followed by agricultural labour activity in case of male in canal irrigated village.

Based on the activity status in the last 24 hours the percentage of non-working population is higher in rain-fed village compared to their usual working status. It could be observed from Table 44 that the percentage of people under casual work and service activity in the last 24 hours was less compared to their usual activity. Very less number of females were engaged in casual work during the last 24 hours.

SUMMARY

East Godavari District (Canal Irrigation) is one of the agriculturally potential districts. Over a period of time area under cultivation of paddy, sugarcane, etc are decreasing. Vizianagaram District is also prominent for agriculture in the costal districts. 80% of area depends on the rains. Literacy rate is higher (65.49) in East Godavari District than in Vizianagaram District (51.7). Cultivators are higher than agricultural labourers in the East Godavari District where as they are in equal proportion in Vizianagaram District. Non-workers are higher than workers in the East Godavari District where as they are of same proportion inVizianagaram District.

The selected village viz., Rapuru is under the canal cultivation where the water for irrigation is available throughout the year. The village profile shows that agricultural labour households are more in the village. In the selected village viz., Gutchimi in rain-fed District, of the total area under cultivation, ¼ is irrigated and ¾ is unirrigated. Village profile shows, cultivator households are more followed by non-agricultural households. Agricltual labour households are very less.

The socio-economic profile of the sample households reveals that majority of the heads of the household and household members are young i.e., below 46 years of age in canal irrigated village whereas in rain-fed the proportion of heads of the households and household members are above 45 years of age. Majority of the heads of the household are illiterates in canal irrigated village where as majority of the household members are illiterate in rain-fed village. The occupational structure of the heads of the households of the sample indicates that agricultural labour household are more in canal irrigated village whereas cultivator households are more in rain-fed village. The occupation of the members of the households reveals the same. In canal irrigated village majority of the heads of the household are not pursuing any secondary occupation where as in rain-fed village majority of the households are pursuing secondary occupation. Considerable proportion is engaged in casual work. It resulted clearly in the low dependency ratio in the rain-fed village. In both the villages majority of the households possess less than or equal to 3 acres of land. But possession of dry land is more in rain-fed than the canal irrigated villages. The cropping differences exist in rain-fed and canal irrigated villages. Janumu is cultivated by less proportion of the households in canal irrigated village where as it is the prominent crop the rain-fed village. In the rain-fed village all the sample households are having electricity for lighting whereas in canal irrigated village still a few households depend on kerosene for lighting. In both the villages majority of the households exclusively depend on firewood for cooking purposes where as the use of LPG for cooking is higher in canal irrigated village. Still some percentage households in rural areas are not having proper dwelling units as of evident from the percentage of households living in thatched houses in both the villages. More than 80 percent of the sample households are poor. Open wells are the major sources of drinking water in both the villages.

FOOTNOTES

1. 'White Colour Ration Card' is issued to the household whose income is low and this is used to get the items under PDS like Rice, Wheat, Dal, Kerosen etc., for low prices.

4

FOOD INTAKE AND NUTRITIONAL STATUS OF THE RURAL HOUSEHOLDS IN ANDHRA PRADESH

INTRODUCTION

This Chapter examines the changes in the nature and quantity of food consumption and nutritional intake of rural households in Andhra Pradesh. National Sample Survey Organisation publishes various reports based on the quinquennial surveys. The data used in this analysis are collected from 50th, 55th, and 61st Rounds of the National Sample Survey (NSS). The Chapter was divided into three sections. Section-I deals with the changes in food consumption with respect to changes in various food items between 1993-94 and 2004-2005. Trends in consumption of food items in Andhra Pradesh are compared with the All-India. Section-II presents the comparative picture of Andhra Pradesh with All India with respect to the nutritional intake between 1993-94 and 2004-05. The third Section presents the district-wise analysis of the consumption of major cereals and pulses during 1993-94 in Andhra Pradesh.

The following are the reports used for the analysis in this Chapter:

1. NSSO (1996): Levels and Pattern of Consumer Expenditure, NSS, 50th Round, (July 1993–June 1994) Report No 402.

2. NSSO (1996): Nutritional Intake in India, NSS, 50th Round, (July 1993 – June 1994) Report No 405.
3. NSSO (1997): Consumption of Some Important Commodities in India, NSS, 50th Round, (July 1993 – June 1994) Report No 404.
4. NSSO (1997): Reported Adequacy of Food Intake in India-1993-94, NSS, 50th Round, (July 1993 – June 1994) Report No 415.
5. NSSO (1998): Ownership of Livestock, Cultivation of Selected Crops and Consumption, NSS, 50th Round, (July 1993 – June 1994) Report No 424.
6. NSSO (2001): Levels and Pattern of Consumer Expenditure in India 1999-2000, NSS, 55th Round, (July 1999 – June 2000) Report No 457.
7. NSSO (2001): Consumption of Some Important Commodities in India 1999-2000, NSS, 55th Round, (July 1999 – June 2000), Report No. 461.
8. NSSO (2001):Reported Adequacy of Food Intake in India 1999-2000, NSS, 55th Round, (July 1999 – June 2000), Report No. 466.
9. NSSO (2001): Nutritional Intake In India 1999-2000, NSS, 55th Round, (July 1999 – June 2000), Report No. 471.
10. NSSO (2001): Differences in Levels of Consumption Among Socio-Economic Groups 1999-2000, NSS, 55th Round, (July 1999 – June 2000), Report No. 472.
11. NSSO (2001):Sources of Household Consumption in India, 1999-2000, NSS, 55th Round, (July 1999 – June 2000), Report No. 474.
12. NSSO(2006): Level and Pattern of Consumer Expenditure in India 2004-2005, NSS, 61st Round, (July 2004 - June 2005), Report No. 508.
13. NSSO (2007): Household Consumption of Various Goods and Services in India, 2004-05, Vol. I: Major States and All-India and Vol. II: Minor States and

Union Territories (Detailed Tables 1-4 only), NSS, 61st Round, (July 2004 - June 2005), Report Nos 509P1 & 509P2.

14. NSSO (2007):Nutritional Intake In India 2004-2005, NSS, 61st Round, (July 2004 - June 2005), Report No. 513.
15. GOAP: Report on Household Consumer Expenditure, State Sample, NSSO, 50th round, (Jul, 1993-June 1994), Directorate of Economics and Statistics, Government of Andhra Pradesh, Hyderabad.

SECTION - I

CHANGES IN FOOD CONSUMPTION

CEREALS

Consumption of cereals-the major constituent of the Indian diet-will be studied using the estimates from per capita quantity of consumption. Analysis of magnitude and trend in food, (Cereals), consumption over a period of time in rural Andhra Pradesh is important in view of its strong implications for food and nutrition security. Such an analysis is necessary due to the failure of expenditure and income based poverty estimates to depict the true picture on food and nutrition security. This section provides evidence, on the magnitude and trends in food consumption in rural Andhra Pradesh.

Table 1 presents per capita monthly consumption of major cereals in rural areas between 1993-94 and 2004-05 both in All-India and Andhra Pradesh. It could be observed that consumption of rice in Andhra Pradesh is higher than All India where as wheat consumption is lower than All India. Bajra and maize also are less consumed in Andhra Pradesh compared to All India. It is clear from the that over the period the consumption of the major cereals has declined at both State and All India levels (See Also Figure 1). The consumption of bajra maize and jowar per person has undergone a noticeable decline in rural areas over the 11 years between 1993-94 and 2004-05.

Table 1
Per capita Monthly Consumption of Major Cereals in Rural Areas During 1993-94 and 2004-05

(Kgs)

	Andhra Pradesh			*All India*		
Major Cereals	*50th Round (1993-94)*	*55th Round (1999-2000)*	*61st Round (2004-2005)*	*50th Round (1993-94)*	*55th Round (1999-2000)*	*61st Round (2004-2005)*
Rice	11.57	11.71	10.95	6.79	6.57	6.38
Wheat	0.19	0.22	0.14	4.32	4.45	4.19
Jowar	0.98	0.44	0.48	0.84	0.50	0.43
Bajra	0.09	0.04	0.04	0.48	0.38	0.39
Maize	0.07	0.02	0.01	0.38	0.32	0.32
All Cereals	13.27	12.65	12.04	13.4	12.72	12.12

Table 2
Monthly Per Capita Consumption of Cereals in the Rural Areas of Andhra Pradesh During 1972-73 and 2004-05

(Kgs)

Item	*27th Round (1972-73)*	*32nd Round (1977-78)*	*38th Round 1983*	*43rd Round (1987-88)*	*50th Round (1993-94)*	*55th Round (1999-00)*	*61st Round (2004-05)*
Rice	8.96	10.86	11.79	11.39	11.57	11.71	10.95
Wheat	0.12	0.11	0.12	0.14	0.19	0.22	0.14
Coarse Cereals	6.17	4.88	3.46	2.82	1.51	0.72	0.94
Cereals	15.25	15.85	15.37	14.35	13.27	12.65	12.04

From the above Table 2 and Figure 2 it is clear that during the period of three decades the increase in the consumption of rice and wheat is less than the decrease in the consumption of coarse cereals which resulted in overall decline in consumption of total cereal consumption in the State.

The NSS data reveal that per capita cereal consumption in India has been declining since the early seventies despite a significant increase in per capita cereal production[1]. The extent of decline in calorie intake has, however, carried significantly between different regions[2]. The sharp fall in cereal consumption has been attributed to changes in consumer preferences from food to non-food items, and within the food

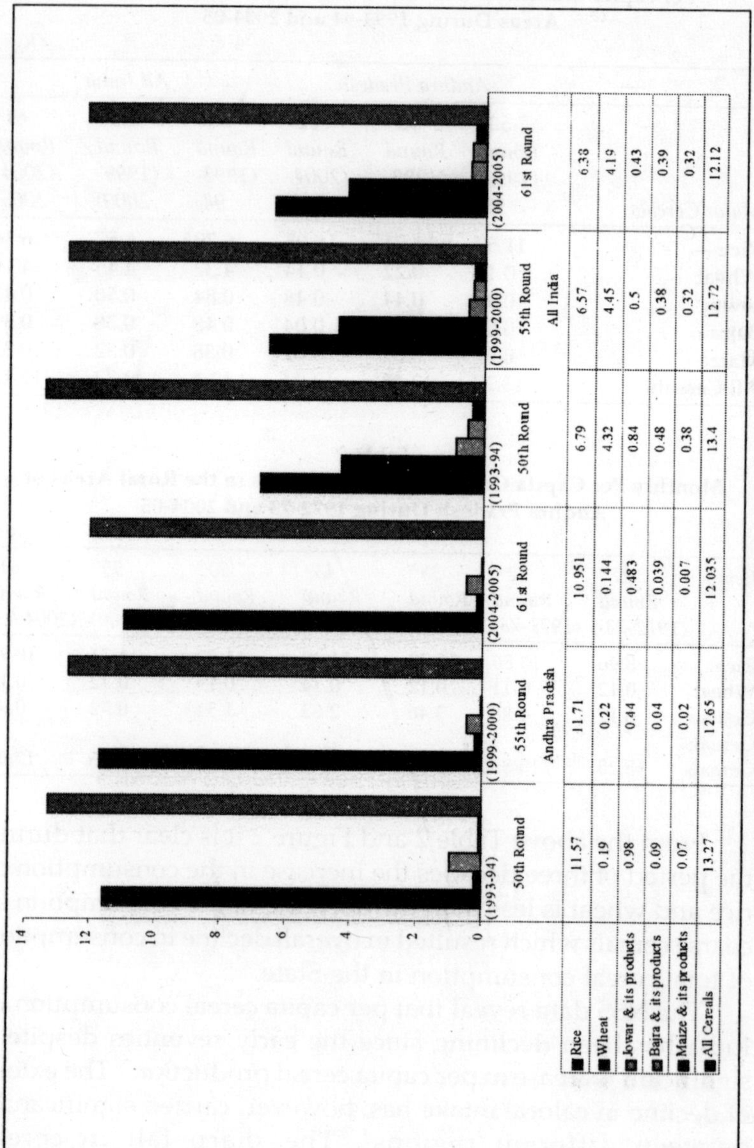

Figure 1: Consumption of Cereals (Kgs./person/month)

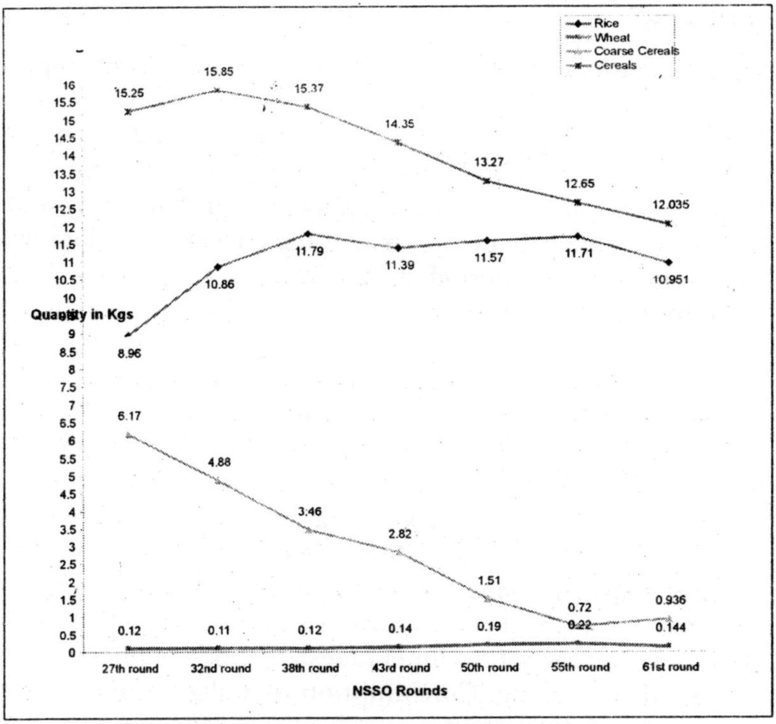

Figure 2: Cereal Consumption in Rural Andhra Pradesh (Kgs/person/month)

group from cereals to non-cereal food items and from 'coarse' to 'fine' cereals[3]. More recently, Rao[4] has shown that the decline in cereal consumption was greater in the rural areas, where improvement in rural infrastructure made other food and non-food items available to the rural households. Rao further observed that a reduction in the intake of cereals on this account should not be taken as deterioration in biological welfare and argues that reduction in hard manual work in agriculture due to farm mechanization might have put downward pressure on the nutritional requirements. The structural factors underlying the changing preferences and their implications for nutritional well-being are little researched and there are severe knowledge gaps.

PULSES

Table 3 presents Andhra Pradesh and All India consumption levels during 1993-94 and 2004-05 of five common varieties of pulses in rural areas. In most cases, there appears to have been a rise in consumption between 1993-94 and 1999-2000 and a subsequent fall. This, however, appears rather unlikely and a more plausible explanation is that the collection of data with the usual reference period of "last 30 days" might have, in the 55th round (1999-2000), been affected by the collection of data with an extra reference period of "last 7 days" immediately before it. This effect appears to have been the strongest in case of such items as pulses, fruits and vegetables, where the monthly consumption of individual items is not as well known to most informants as it is in case of cereals. If one assumes, therefore, that the 1999-2000 data are not comparable with those of the other years, the picture is simplified, with the figures showing a small reduction in per capita consumption for most varieties of pulses during 1993-94 and 2004-05 at All India level. In case of Andhra Pradesh the consumption of arhar reported increasing. Consumption of pulses appears to be getting more diversified.

Table 3
Per capita Monthly Consumption of Major Pulses in Rural Areas During 1993-94 and 2004-05

(Kgs)

	Andhra Pradesh			*All India*		
Major Pulses	*50th Round (1993-94)*	*55th Round (1999-2000)*	*61st Round (2004-2005)*	*50th Round (1993-94)*	*55th Round (1999-2000)*	*61st Round (2004-2005)*
Arhar	0.35	0.39	0.424	0.24	0.23	0.21
Moong	0.18	0.12	0.089	0.10	0.10	0.09
Masur	0.02	-	0.008	0.12	0.14	0.11
Urd	0.09	0.11	0.104	0.10	0.09	0.08
Gram (Split)	0.05	0.07	0.050	0.06	0.08	0.06
All Pulses & Pulse Products	0.70	0.73	0.702	0.76	0.84	0.71

The Figure 3 shows the quantity of consumption of pulses is lower in Andhra Pradesh than All India. In case of arhar the per capita monthly consumption is presumably higher in Andhra Pradesh than All India. The consumption of masur is almost negligible in Andhra Pradesh compared to All India. During 1993-94 the per capita monthly consumption of moong was higher compared to the All India, but gradually the consumption declined to the All India level.

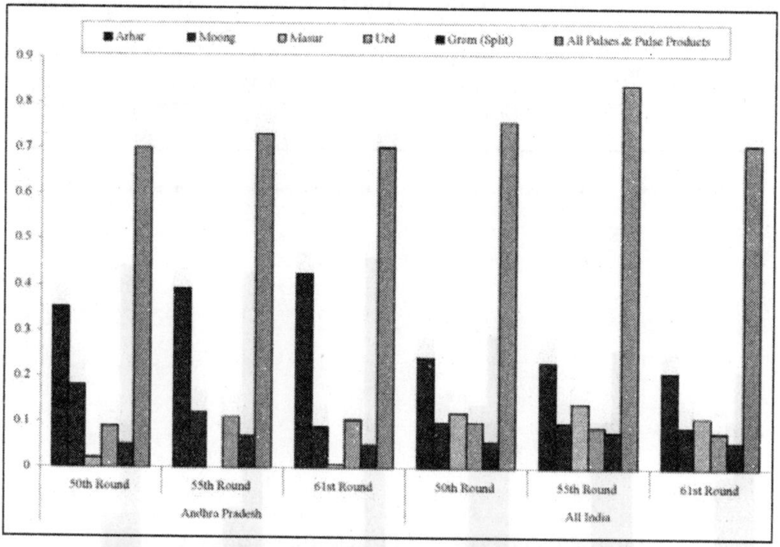

Figure 3: Consumption of Pulses (Kgs/person/month)

MILK, EGGS, FISH & MEAT

There appears to have been a slight fall in per capita consumption of "milk (liquid)" in rural All India and a slight rise in Andhra Pradesh during 1993-94 and 2004-05 (Table 4)[5]. Egg consumption has apparently increased in the 11 years in both Andhra Pradesh and All India. Per capita consumption of goat meat and mutton has definitely declined, more so in Andhra Pradesh. The increase in per capita consumption levels of chicken appears to be increased at All India but is increased significantly in Andhra Pradesh. Per capita consumption of chicken has outstripped goat meat and mutton in rural India.

Table 4
Per capita Monthly Consumption of Milk, Eggs, Fish & Meat During 1993-94 and 2004-05

NSSO Rounds	*Andhra Pradesh (rural)*			*All India (rural)*		
	50th Round (1993-94)	*55th Round (1999-2000)*	*61st Round (2004-2005)*	*50th Round (1993-94)*	*55th Round (1999-2000)*	*61st Round (2004-2005)*
Milk(Litres)	2.62	2.87	3.051	3.94	3.79	3.87
Eggs(No.)	1.44	2.07	2.251	0.64	1.09	1.01
Fish (Kg.)	0.11	0.18	0.071	0.18	0.21	0.201
Goat Meat/ Mutton(Kg.)	0.13	0.10	0.086	0.06	0.07	0.047
Chicken (Kg.)	0.05	0.10	0.136	0.02	0.04	0.050

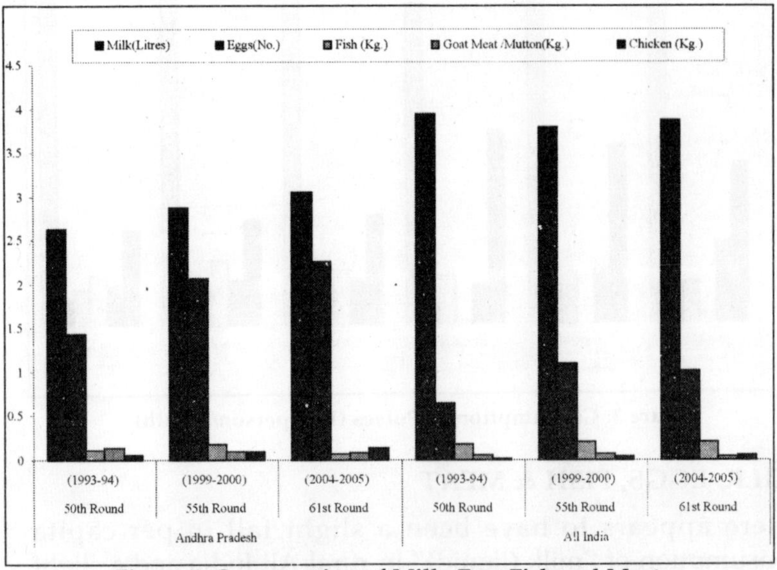

Figure 4: Consumption of Milk, Egg, Fish and Meat

EDIBLE OILS

Per capita consumption of edible oil has definitely been rising over the 11 years following 1993-94. Table 5 shows the extent of increase in rural All India and in Andhra Pradesh. In All

India rural areas, there has been a fall of about 50 gm per person per month in the consumption of groundnut oil, offset by a corresponding rise for mustard oil. In Andhra Pradesh the decline in per capita consumption of groundnut oil is about 140 gm per month, which is more than the rise in mustard oil and vanaspati consumption. In both Andhra Pradesh and All

Table 5
Per Capita Monthly Consumption of Edible Oil in Rural Areas Between 1993-94 and 2004-05

(Kgs)

	Andhra Pradesh			*All India*		
NSSO Rounds	*50th Round (1993-94)*	*55th Round (1999-2000)*	*61st Round (2004-2005)*	*50th Round (1993-94)*	*55th Round (1999-2000)*	*61st Round (2004-2005)*
Groundnut Oil	0.36	0.29	0.239	0.12	0.12	0.07
Mustard Oil	-	-	0.001	0.17	0.24	0.22
Vanaspati	-	-	0.001	0.03	0.04	0.03
Edible Oil (Other)	-	0.17	0.312	0.05	0.09	0.14
Edible Oil (All)	-	0.46	0.554	0.37	0.50	0.48

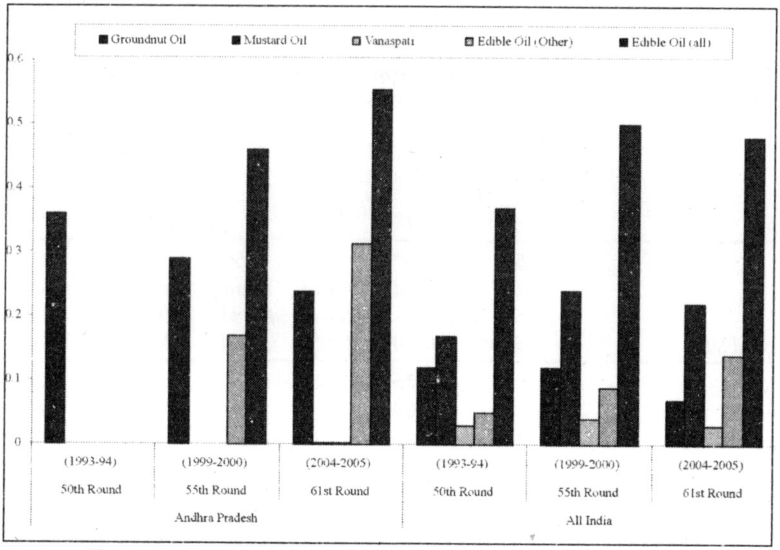

Figure 5: Consumption of Edible Oils (Kgs/person/month)

India, per capita consumption of oil other than groundnut oil, mustard oil, vanaspati and has more than doubled, increasing steadily both before and after 1999-2000. Such oil would include sunflower oil, soyabean oil, other vegetable oils, rice bran oil, palm oil etc.

VEGETABLES

Table 6 shows levels of consumption of some common vegetables between 1993-94 and 2004-05. The per capita consumption levels of the vegetables listed have increased except brinjal. Per capita monthly consumption of potato, cauliflower, cabbage is lower in Andhra Pradesh than All India. Consumption of onions, tomatoes per person per month is higher in Andhra Pradesh than All India. For all the vegetables in All India, potatoes, brinjal, oinion, cauliflowers, cabbages and tomatoes, the 55th round estimates (1999-2000) suggest an increase in per capita consumption in the period before 1999-2000 and a fall subsequently, which is unlikely. In Andhra Pradesh except potato and brinjal all the other vegetables reported an increase.

Table 6
Per Capita Monthly Consumption of Common Vegetables in Rural During 1993-94 and 2004-05

(Kgs)

	Andhra Pradesh (rural)			*All India (rural)*		
Vegetables	*50th Round (1993-94)*	*55th Round (1999-2000)*	*61st Round (2004-2005)*	*50th Round (1993-94)*	*55th Round (1999-2000)*	*61st Round (2004-2005)*
Potato	0.17	0.26	0.223	1.24	1.61	1.33
Onion	0.60	0.69	0.719	0.46	0.58	0.56
Brinjal	0.4	0.47	0.402	0.41	0.39	0.34
Cauliflower	0.06	-	0.021	0.16	0.19	0.18
Cabbage	0.05	0.08	0.085	0.15	0.18	0.17
Tomato	0.47	0.57	0.634	0.29	0.35	0.34

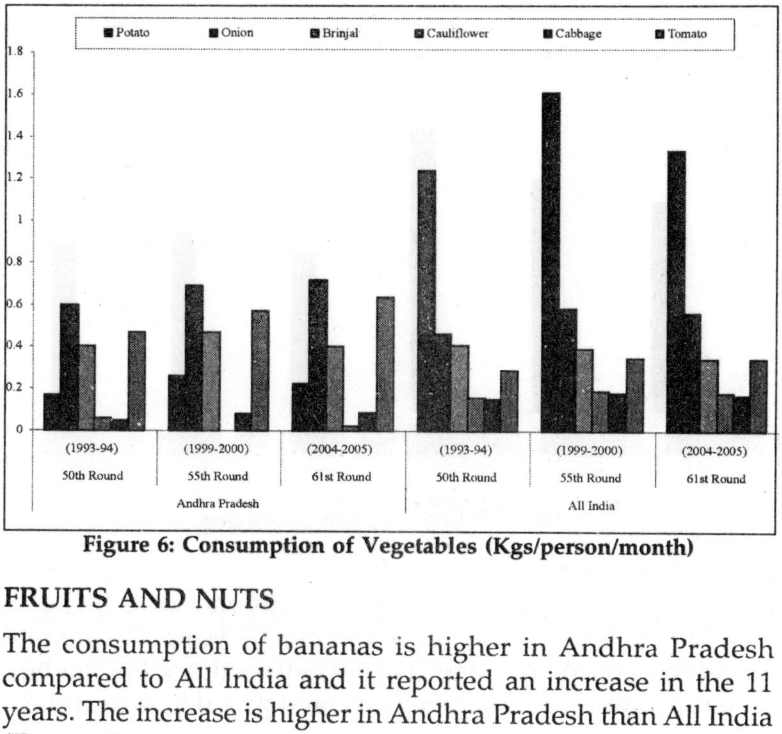

Figure 6: Consumption of Vegetables (Kgs/person/month)

FRUITS AND NUTS

The consumption of bananas is higher in Andhra Pradesh compared to All India and it reported an increase in the 11 years. The increase is higher in Andhra Pradesh than All India (Figure 7).

Table 7
Per Capita Monthly Consumption of Common Fruits & Nuts in Rural Areas Between 1993-94 and 2004-05

	Andhra Pradesh			*All India*		
Fruits & Nuts	*50th Round (1993-94)*	*55th Round (1999-2000)*	*61st Round (2004-2005)*	*50th Round (1993-94)*	*55th Round (1999-2000)*	*61st Round (2004-2005)*
Banana (No.)	2.85	3.17	3.913	2.20	2.48	2.37
Coconut (No.)	0.22	0.22	0.269	0.32	0.37	0.35
Mango (Kg.)	0.10	0.06	0.152	0.06	0.10	0.09
Apple (Kg.)	0.01	-	0.019	0.03	-	0.03
Groundnut (Kg.)	0.05	0.03	0.059	0.03	0.05	0.05

The per capita monthly consumption of coconut and apple is higher in All India than Andhra Pradesh where as per capita

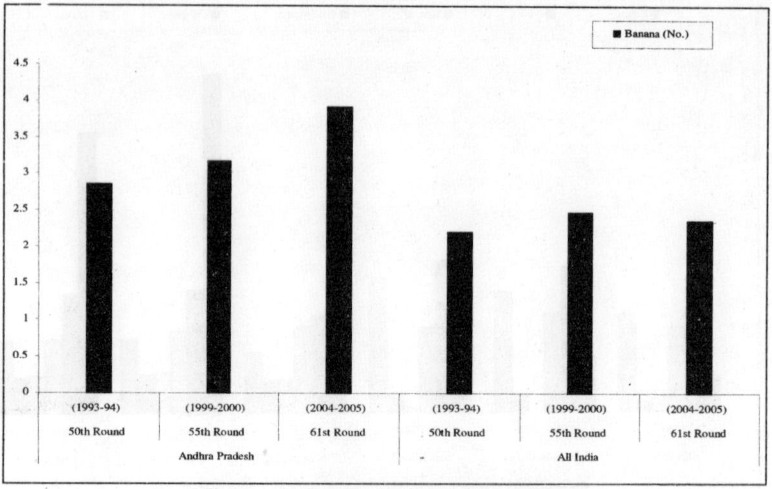

Figure 7: Consumption of Bananas

monthly consumption of mango and groundnut is higher in Andhra Pradesh than All India. Over the 11 years consumption of coconut has increased both in All India and Andhra Pradesh. The consumption of mango, apple and groundnut recorded a

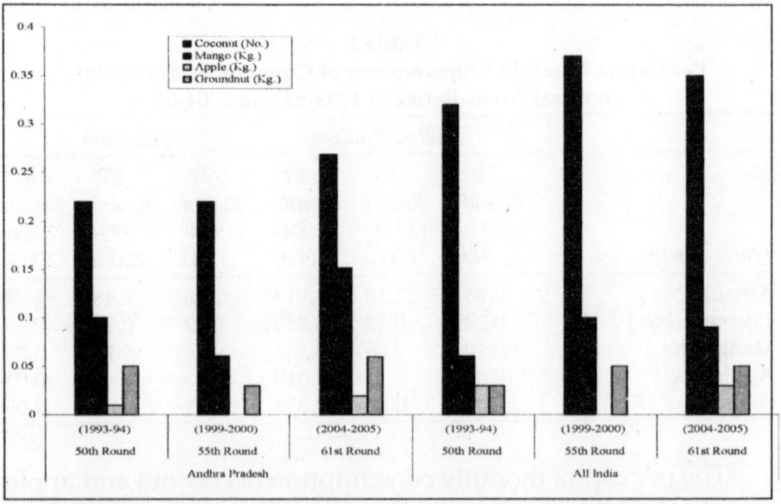

Figure 8: Consumption of Coconut, Mango, Apple Ground nut

decrease in 1999-2000 and then increased in 2004-05 in Andhra Pradesh. From Figure 8 it could also be observed that the consumption of mango increased in 1999-2000 and then decreased in 2004-05, which is quite opposite scenario of Andhra Pradesh.

SECTION – II

NUTRITION INTAKE

The quantity of consumption of different food items are converted into nutritional values which are presented in the NSS reports. The following table presents the per capita and per consumer unit intake of calories, proteins and fats per diem.

PER CAPITA PER DIEM NUTRITIONAL INTAKE

From Table 8 it is evident that the average of intake of calorie, and protein per capita per diem over the period of time is gradually declining at State level as well as national level. The per capita per diem consumption of fats recorded an increase both at state level as well as national level. But the increase is higher in Andhra Pradesh than All India.

Table 8
Per Capita Per diem Intake of Calorie, Protein and Fat in Rural Areas

NSSO Rounds	*Andhra Pradesh*			*All India*		
	Calorie (K.Cal)	*Protein (gms.)*	*Fat (gms.)*	*Calorie (K.Cal)*	*Protein (gms.)*	*Fat (gms.)*
50th Round (1993-94)	2052	50.8	27.2	2153	60.2	31.4
55th Round (1999-2000)	2021	49.4	29.5	2149	59.1	36.1
61st Round (2004-2005)	1995	49.8	33.5	2047	57.0	35.5

PER CONSUMER UNIT PER DIEM NUTRITIONAL INTAKE

The per consumer unit per diem average intake of calorie, protein, and fat is presented in Table 9. Similar trend of per capita per diem intake could also be observed. But the interesting thing to notice is that the decline is higher during

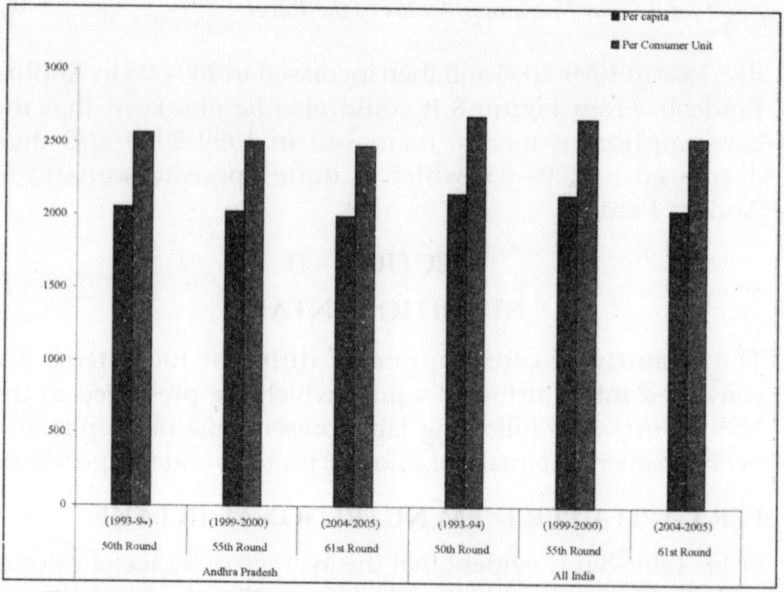

Figure 9: Per Capita & Per Consumer Unit Calorie Intake (K.Cal)

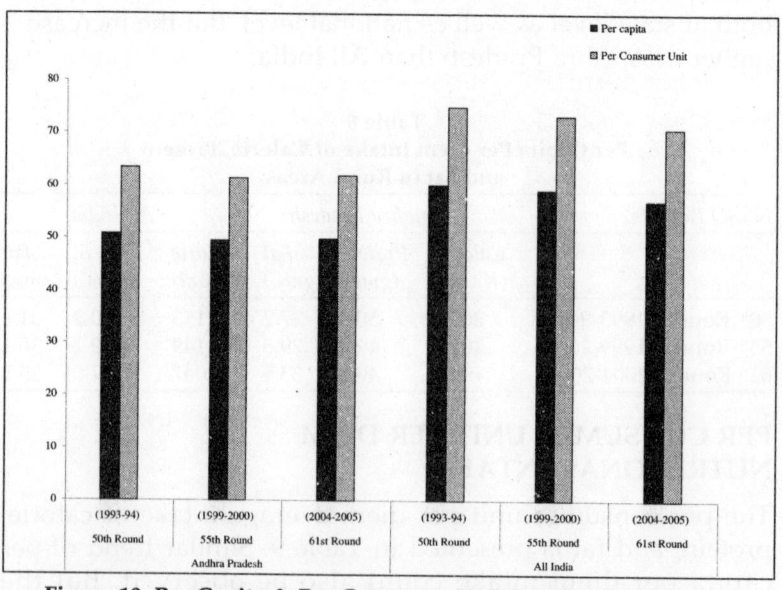

Figure 10: Per Capita & Per Consumer Unit Protein Intake (gms.)

50th–55th rounds than during 55th-60th rounds. Another point to notice is either the case of per capita or per consumer unit, at both state and national levels the per diem intake of calorie is less than the norm i.e., 2700

Table 9
Per Consumer Unit Per diem Intake of Calorie, Protein and Fat in Rural Area

NSSO Rounds	*Andhra Pradesh*			*All India*		
	Calorie (K.Cal)	*Protein (g)*	*Fat (g)*	*Calorie (K.Cal)*	*Protein (g)*	*Fat (g)*
50th Round(1993-94)	2559	63.4	34.0	2683	75.0	64.2
55th Round(1999-2000)	2503	61.2	36.5	2668	73.4	44.9
61st Round (2004-2005)	2475	61.8	41.6	2540	70.8	44.0

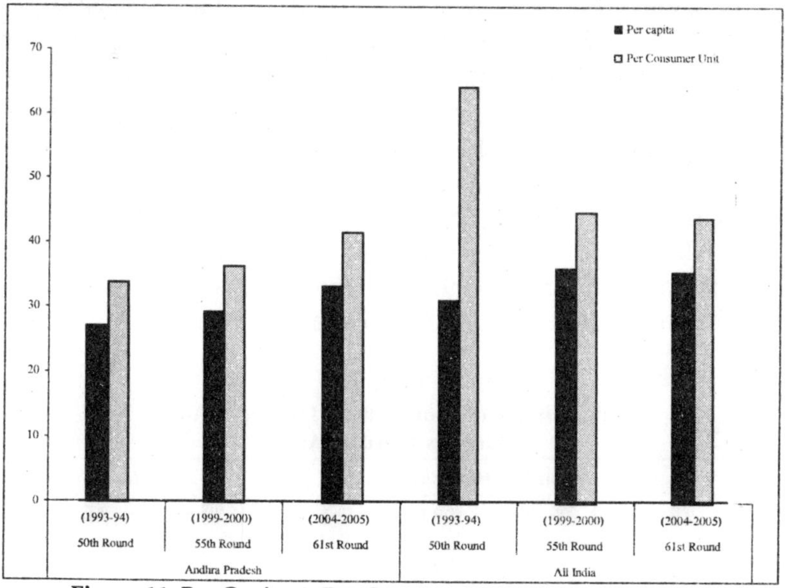

Figure 11: Per Capita & Per Consumer Unit Fat Intake (gms.)

SHARE OF CEREALS IN THE TOTAL INTAKE OF CALORIE

The percentage share of contribution of cereals to the total calorie intake is gradually decreasing and the decrease is by 5 percentage points in Andhra Pradesh where as the decrease is nearly 3.5 points at All India level.

Table 10
Percentage of Calorie from Cereals in Rural Areas

NSSO Rounds	*Andhra Pradesh*		*All India*	
	Cereals	*Other Food*	*Cereals*	*Other Food*
50th Round(1993-94)	74.42	25.58	71.01	28.99
55th Round(1999-2000)	72.06	27.94	67.55	32.45
61st Round (2004-2005)	69.44	30.56	67.54	32.31

SHARE OF DIFFERENT FOOD ITEMS IN THE TOTAL INTAKE OF PROTEIN

The percentage contribution of cereals to the average intake of protein in Andhra Pradesh was 67 percent during 1993-94, which came down to 62 5 in 2004-05. At the all India level it was 69 percent during1993-94 and came down to 67 percent in 2004-05. However, the percentage of total intake of protein derived from other types of food groups, especially milk, and milk products showed an increasing trend both at State level and All India level. Pulses as a sources of protein came next to the cereals, but during 1999-2000 there was a slight increase in their contribution but in 2004-05 again fell down.

Table 11
Percentage of Protein from Different Food Groups in Rural Areas

	Andhra Pradesh				*All India*			
NSSO Rounds	*Cereals*	*Pulses*	*Milk & Milk Products*	*Egg, Fish & Meat*	*Cereals*	*Pulses*	*Milk & Milk Products*	*Egg, Fish & Meat*
50th Round (1993-94)	67.92	10.63	7.08	5.70	69.42	9.76	8.81	3.66
55th Round (1999-2000)	65.58	11.17	8.00	6.80	67.43	10.91	9.19	4.04
61st Round (2004-2005)	62.14	10.68	8.47	5.91	66.37	9.47	9.28	3.98

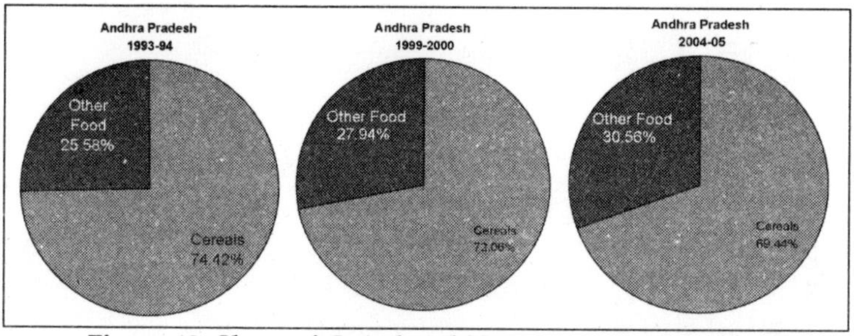

Figure 12: Share of Cereal and Non-Cereal Food in Total Calorie Intake–Andhra Pradesh

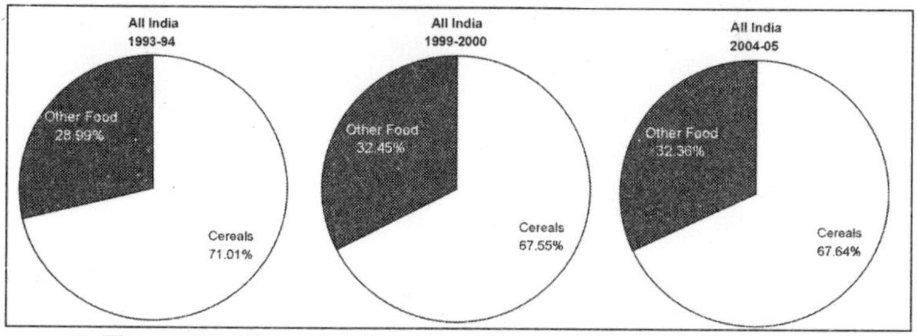

Figure 13: Share of Cereal and Non-Cereal Food in Total Calorie Intake –All India

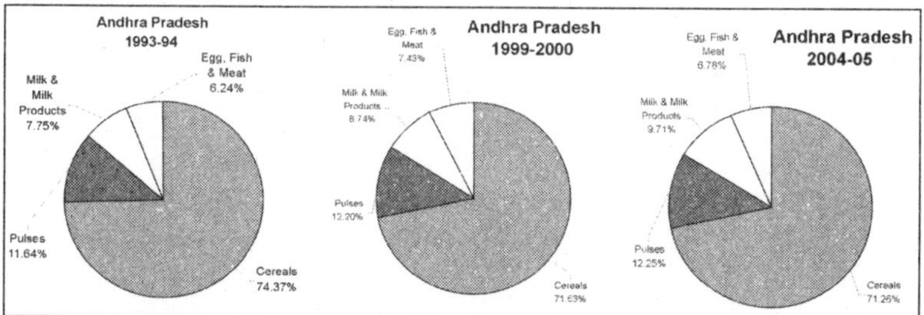

Figure 14: Share of Different Food in Total Calorie Intake–Andhra Pradesh

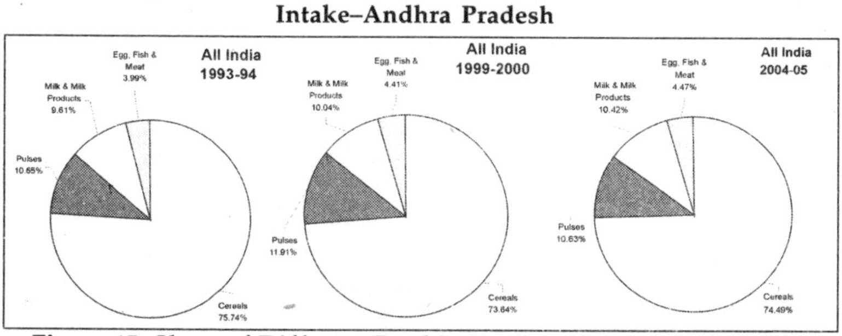

Figure 15: Share of Different Food in Total Calorie Intake–All India

Table 12
Percentage Breakup of Calorie Intake Over Different Food Groups in Rural Area

NSSO Rounds	*Andhra Pradesh*									*All India*								
	I	II	III	IV	V	VI	VII	VIII	IX	I	II	III	IV	V	VI	VII	VIII	IX
50th Round (1993-94)	74.43	0.88	3.26	4.76	2.00	1.00	4.37	3.88	3.41	71.03	2.65	4.88	4.92	2.02	0.68	6.15	5.34	2.41
55th Round (1999-2000)	72.06	1.12	3.21	5.12	1.94	1.13	4.84	6.92	3.66	67.55	3.25	5.14	5.46	1.97	0.77	6.17	7.37	2.32
61st Round (2004-2005)	69.44	1.11	3.11	5.02	2.44	0.97	5.22	8.39	4.32	67.54	2.95	4.78	4.98	2.23	0.76	6.42	7.36	2.98

DISTRIBUTION OF TOTAL CALORIE INTAKE OF DIFFERENT FOOD GROUPS

Table 12 presents the distribution of total calorie intake over nine different food groups. As the calorie intake is concerned, the major source of energy was cereals (Group I). Next comes in percentage of contribution were oils and fats (food group VIII) followed by milk and milk products (food group VII), pulses, nuts and oils seeds (food group IV) and sugar and honey (food group III) at both Andhra Pradesh and All India level[6].

NUMBER OF MEALS PER DAY

The average number of meals taken per day at home, and away from home is provided in Table 13 and Table 14. It could be observed that the number of meals consumed on an average per person per day was higher in Andhra Pradesh compared to All-India and the average declined from 2.72 in 1993-94 to 2.66 in 2004-05.

Table 13
Average Number of Meals Consumed Per Person Per Day at Home[7]

NSSO Rounds	*Andhra Pradesh*	*All India*
50th Round(1993-94)	2.72	2.38
55th Round(1999-2000)	2.74	2.14
61st Round (2004-2005)	2.66	2.38

Table 14
No. of Meals Taken Outside Household During Last 30 days of the Survey

NSSO Rounds	*Andhra Pradesh*		*All India*	
	Free	*Payment*	*Free*	*Payment*
50th Round(1993-94)	9	1	6	1
55th Round(1999-2000)	7	1	6	1
61st Round (2004-2005)	14	1	11	1

The number free meals taken outside the home also increased particularly in the State of Andhra Pradesh signifies the important role played by the welfare programmes like

'Mid-day Meals for School Children'. Table 15 presents the source of food grains from PDS, Home Grown and Purchased. It is evident from the Table that the consumption of rice from home grown quantity is more in rural Andhra Pradesh and also the contribution of PDS towards the rice supply is considerable. The supply of wheat, edible oils etc., should be increased in order to improve the nutritional status of the rural households.

Table 15
Quantity of Per Capita Monthly Consumption of Specific Items from Different Sources in Andhra Pradesh During 1993-94

(Kgs)

Item	*Source*			
	PDS	*Home Grown Stock*	*Other*	*Total*
Rice	2.58	9.17	2.28	14.16
Wheat	0.28	004	0.23	0.51
All Edible Oils	0.01	0.01	0.40	0.42
Sugar	0.33	-	0.18	0.51

Andhra Pradesh: District-wise Analysis-1993-94

Table 16 and Table 17 present the data on per capita monthly consumption of cereals and pulses in 1993-94. It could be observed that there exits variations at district level. Rice, wheat and jowar are the common cereal food in all districts. Small millets are consumed only in one district. Barly was not at all the consumed in any district. Consumption of maize is observed in Telangana region where as the consumption of bajra and ragi is observed in Costal and Rayalaseema Regions. With respect to pulses arhar, gram (split gram), moong and urd are the common verities consumed in all districts. Consumption of masure could be observed in Telangana Districts. Consumption of soyabeen is meager. Very less quantities of consumption of other pulses could be found in few districts. Therefore, it could be said that the local availability influences the consumption of food items.

Table 16

District-Wise Monthly Per Capita Consumption of Cereals in Rural Andhra Pradesh During 1993-94

(Kgs)

District	Rice	Wheat	Jowar	Bajra	Maize	Small Millets	Ragi	Total Cereals
Srikakulam	12.60	0.09	0.01	0.03	-	-	1.86	14.60
Vizianagaram	10.83	0.12	-	0.17	-	-	1.60	12.72
Visakhapatnam	9.76	0.31	0.07	0.05	-	-	1.06	11.23
East Godavari	11.04	0.32	0.01	0.03	-	-	0.01	11.41
West Godavari	13.41	0.19	-	-	-	-	0.03	13.63
Krishna	12.61	0.11	0.02	-	-	-	-	12.74
Guntur	11.67	0.11	-	-	-	-	-	11.79
Prakasham	12.37	0.07	0.95	0.22	-	-	0.90	14.51
Nellore	11.06	0.15	-	-	-	-	-	11.21
Chittoor	11.94	0.21	-	-	-	-	0.61	12.76
Cuddapah	11.82	0.31	0.49	0.04	-	-	0.28	12.94
Anantapur	7.8	0.28	0.85	0.08	-	-	2.01	11.02
Kurnool	9.12	0.15	3.40	0.09	-	0.21	-	12.97
Mahboobnagar	9.84	0.15	3.17	0.03	-	-	0.13	13.86
Rangareddy	8.94	0.22	2.02	-	-	-	0.1	11.37
Hyderabad	-	-	-	-		-	-	-
Medak	7.32	0.20	3.99	-	0.05	-	0.11	11.67
Nizamabad	14.09	0.08	0.50	-	-	-	-	14.68
Adilabad	7.2	0.50	5.65	-	0.45	-	-	13.86
Karimnagar	13.02	0.34	-	-	0.19	-	-	13.55
Warangal	12.18	0.12	0.01	-	-	-	-	12.31
Khammam	10.29	0.34	0.43	-	0.12	-	-	11.18
Nalgonda	12.54	0.06	0.16	0.07	-	-	-	12.83

Source: Report on Household Consumer Expenditure, NSS 50th Rond, State Sample, Directorate of Economics & Statistics, Government of Andhra Pradesh.

Table 17

District-Wise Monthly Per Capita Consumption of Pulses in Rural Andhra Pradesh During 1993-94

(Kgs)

District	*Arhar*	*Gram (Split Gram)*	*Moong*	*Masur*	*Urd*	*Soyabeen*	*Other Pulses*	*Total Pulses*
Srikakulam	0.10	-	0.24	-	0.07	-	-	0.46
Vizianagaram	0.17	0.05	0.19	-	0.08	-	-	0.52
Visakhapatnam	0.27	0.08	0.16	-	0.13	-	-	0.68
East Godavari	0.10	0.05	0.20	-	0.11	-	-	0.51
West Godavari	0.29	0.06	0.07	-	0.23	-	-	0.68
Krishna	0.27	0.04	0.06	-	0.23	-	-	0.61
Guntur	0.36	0.01	0.08	-	0.10	-	-	0.55
Prakasham	0.41	0.07	0.06	-	0.12	-	-	0.65
Nellore	0.26	0.21	0.41	-	0.25	-	-	1.13
Chittoor	0.34	0.05	0.03	-	0.07	-	-	0.05
Cuddapah	0.47	0.07	-	-	0.10	-	0.01	0.75
Anantapur	0.58	0.02	0.01	-	0.01	0.02	0.01	0.65
Kurnool	0.57	0.04	0.01	-	0.02	-	-	0.67
Mahboobnagar	0.42	0.04	0.04	0.01	0.01	-	0.01	0.54
Rangareddy	0.33	0.06	0.16	0.03	-	-	-	0.59
Hyderabad	0.39	0.07	0.10	0.08	0.10	-	-	0.76
Medak	0.32	0.06	0.20	0.03	-	-	-	0.61
Nizamabad	0.59	0.13	0.56	0.01	0.39	-	-	1.67
Adilabad	0.59	0.01	0.26	0.03	0.02	-	-	0.91
Karimnagar	0.16	-	0.36	0.06	0.04	-	0.01	0.66
Warangal	0.21	0.03	0.29	0.04	-	-	-	0.57
Khammam	0.44	0.03	0.10	0.01	0.05	-	0.01	0.68
Nalgonda	0.33-	-	0.15	-	0.01	-	-	0.50

Source: Report on Household Consumer Expenditure, NSS 50th Rond, State Sample, Directorate of Economics & Statistics, Government of Andhra Pradesh. 4. Public Distribution System (PDS) in India

PDS in India is quite unique in terms of the extent and intensity of its coverage. With a network of about 4.75 lakh Fair Price Shops (FPS) in 2004, PDS is possibly the largest distribution network of its type in the world. It is a major instrument in the government's anti-poverty programme and serves as a safety net for the poor. Responding to criticisms that the PDS has an urban bias and fails to serve the poor, the government introduced in June, 1997 the targeted PDS (TPDS) which distinguished between "below the poverty line" (BPL) and "above the poverty line" (APL) families in setting the quantity and issue price of the subsidised food grain items. In a further tightening of the PDS, the government introduced on December 25, 2000, the "Antyodaya Anna Yojana" (AAY) scheme that makes the TPDS more focussed by targeting the very poor, i.e. the destitute, who formed a population of one crore families out of a total of 6.52 crore BPL families covered under TPDS.

Table 18
Calorie Share of PDS Items in Rural Indian Households

State	*All Households*	
	NSS 50th Round (1993/94)	*NSS 55th Round (1999/00)*
Andhra Pradesh	0.177	0.153
Assam	0.051	0.058
Bihar	0.022	0.022
Gujarat	0.093	0.076
Haryana	0.025	0.019
Himachal Pradesh	0.143	0.140
Karnataka	0.084	0.111
Kerala	0.303	0.280
Madhya Pradesh	0.038	0.042
Maharashtra	0.070	0.085
Orissa	0.021	0.112
Punjab	0.018	0.014
Rajasthan	0.067	0.024
Tamil Nadu	0.157	0.242
Uttar Pradesh	0.027	0.026
West Bengal	0.028	0.035
All India	0.071	0.078

The role of the PDS has figured prominently in discussions on the economic reforms undertaken in India in the 1990s. Table 18 provides some evidence on this issue by reporting the share of the household's intake of calories that is contributed by the PDS.

Table 18 shows that the importance of the PDS in supplying inexpensive calories to the household varies sharply between the constituent states of the Indian Union. For example, a much larger share of the total calorie intake is supplied through the PDS in the southern states, especially Kerala and Tamil Nadu, than in the northern states such as Punjab, Rajasthan, Haryana and Bihar.

Food Security and Nutritional Security

Food security in India has essentially meant food grain security, meeting the requirements of energy and protein. As stressed earlier, for nutrition security, food production should ensure availability of diverse foods which can enhance the nutritional content including micro nutrients. Nutrition security is thus a broader term. It includes within it food grain security but goes beyond it. Under-nourishment has a deleterious effect on the life of people. Malnourished children grow up to become adults unable to operate at full potential. Development economics and policy makers need to take into account the effects of nutritional and health care deprivation on human productivity. The links between nutritional status and the capacity for work have not so far been adequately incorporated in growth models. Poor nutrition and under nourishment result in low productivity leading to low wages which in turn results in poor nutrition intake. Thus a vicious cycle is set in motion. This has been described by one writer as 'poverty trap'.

Ensuring nutrition security requires attention on programmes aimed at–

(a) Enhancing food grain production with a nutritional orientation;

(b) Improving the food distribution system so that the poor have access to food grain at affordable prices;

(c) Augmenting the purchasing power of the poor through special schemes in times of stress and vulnerability; and

(d) Focusing on direct nutrition intervention programmes to address the needs of vulnerable groups.

SUMMARY

Consumption of rice in Andhra Pradesh is higher than All India where as wheat consumption is lower than All India. Bajra and maize also less consumed in Andhra Pradesh compared to All India. over the period consumption of the major cereals declined at both State and All India levels. Consumption of jowar, bajra and maize per person has also undergone a noticeable decline in rural areas over the eleven years between 1993-94 and 2004-05.

There is a shift in food consumption throughout the 1990s from Cereals, which are a source of cheap calories, to more expensive calorie sources such as Meat, Fish and Eggs and Fruits/Vegetables, resulted in a decline in calorie intake. Calorie share of "Other Cereals", such as barley, maize and tapioca, recorded large decline in rural areas over this period.

Interesting thing to notice is that the decline is higher during 50th–55th rounds than during 55th-60th rounds. Both state and national levels the per diem intake of calorie is less than the norm i.e., 2700.

Decline in cereal consumption, and an increase in the prevalence of undernourishment over the period, 1987/88–2001/2002 suggests that there is a need for a reassessment of the current strategy of directing the TPDS exclusively at households "below the poverty line" (BPL).

Number of free meals taken outside the home also increased particularly in the Andhra Pradesh signifies the important role played by the welfare programmes like 'Mid-day Meals for School Children'.

Variation in the consumption of cereals and pulses among various districts of Andhra Pradesh during 1993-94 clearly indicated the influence of local availability of certain cereals and pulses. Therefore, if the cultivation of some verities of cereals or pulses is encouraged, it will increase the consumption of those items.

FOOTNOTES

1. Radhakrishna, R., and C. Ravi (1992): Effects of Growth, Relative Price and Preference on Food and Nutrition, *Indian Economic Review*, 27 (Special Number), 303-323.

   Rao, C.H.H. (2000): Declining Demand for Foodgrains in Rural India: Causes and Implications, *Economic and Political Weekly*, January 2.
2. P.G.K. Panikar (1980): Inter-Regional Variations in Calorie Intake, *Economic and Political Weekly*, Special No., October, Vol. XV, Nos. 41, 42 & 43.
3. Radhakrishna, R., and C. Ravi (1992): ibid
4. Rao, C.H.H. (2000): ibid
5. Note that consumption of milk products such as curd and butter prepared from milk at home is accounted against "milk (liquid)" by convention. This means that if a household that used to prepare the butter it consumed switches to purchase of butter from the market, aggregate consumption of "milk (liquid)" would fall.
6. In NSSO reports information about all these food groups and items under each group was provided
7. Average no of meals per day per person = No. of meals during the last 30 days/(average size of the household*30)

5

FOOD INTAKE OF SAMPLE HOUSEHOLDS

INTRODUCTION

The food habits and inequalities in the food intake of the sample households are analysed in this Chapter. Food preparation timings, items prepared for the diet during morning cooking and evening cooking are analysed at the household level. General food habits like drinking coffee/tea, having tiffen at the breakfast, or having meals in the morning instead of breakfast, or taking tiffen in the evening in stead of dinner are analysed at the individual level to capture the intra-household differences. Nature of inequality has been assessed by comparing the values of mean, standard deviation and skewness of various food items. For an easy understanding of the inequalities in the consumption of food items, graphical presentation was also done by using the histogram.

Eating Habits

'Indian Food Intake Survey' is a study aimed at planners as well as manufacturers of food products. i-FIS has been carried out by Protein Foods and Nutrition Development Association of India (PFNDAI) and Pathfinders: India, a leading Market Research Agency to understand the eating habits of people across the country: What do they eat? How much do they eat? How much of their food intake is constituted by various types of food? How much of the food consumed is packaged foods and what proportion is freshly prepared food? How do they view the increasing number of nutraceuticals available on the shop shelves? How do all these vary by geographies within the country, by socio-cultural and socio economic backgrounds and by a plethora of other variables? These and innumerable other similar questions are answered by the study. "i-FIS has been carried out on pan-India coverage. Done in two phases, the first phase of the study covered North and South zones, while the second phase covered the East and West zones. The current round of the study is representative of all towns with a population of 100,000 or above. Using a stratified sampling method, these class of towns have been represented a sample of nearly 5500 households drawn from by 23 towns across the length and breadth of the country. The data collection for the study followed the Yesterday Consumption Method.

When it comes to the eating habits of people across the country, we as a nation are far out of balance. At least, that's what the i-FIS would make us believe: South Indians are more likely to be non-vegetarians than North Indians. However, highest percentage of non-vegetarians is from East probably due to fish consumption, whereas West has about equal vegetarians and non-vegetarians. On an average the North Indians eat twice the amount of cereals compared to South Indians, the major cereal being wheat. West Indians also consume about the similar amounts, but a sizeable amount of rice is also consumed with wheat. East Indians consume moderate amount of cereals and the major cereal is rice. Milk consumption is mostly by adding to tea, the all-India average being almost ¾ through tea. West is leading there with over 80%. North Indians lead in drinking plain milk. Most milk is procured loose whereas only about 20% is packaged in different regions of India. There are more non-vegetarian households in the lower socio-economic strata as compared to the upper ones. There are almost half the households in South, West and East consuming eggs. South Indians consume most of the 'ready made' cooking powders available on the retail shelves. Among the spice powders, turmeric and chili powders are consumed all over India, but cumin powders are more popular in East and West, whereas garam masala is most used in North. Today, more and more families, both adults as well as children are enjoying chocolates at home. Around twice the proportion of North Indians rarely drink coffee as compared to the South Indians who rarely drink tea. West and East Indians drink mostly tea.

No food in itself is good or bad. It is the amount of food consumed and the method of preparation that counts. For example Rice and Wheat are the sources of carbohydrates. Steamed rice is good for low fat than rotis prepared with oil and ghee. Similarly dry rotis have less than biryani. Fat comes form the method of preparation used.

Therefore the nutritional value of the food taken by the people is influenced by many issues. However, in this Chapter an attempt is made to document the information on the food preparation and consumption habits of the sample households and household members.

INTER HOUSEHOLD DIFFERENCES IN THE ITEMS PREPARED UNDER VARIOUS MEALS

Generally all the households prepare food daily twice morning and evening. Table 1 and Table 2 present the details of the timing of food preparation during morning and evening. It could be observed that the time of cooking ranges from 6 A. M. to 12 noon in the morning in canal irrigated village where as it ranges from 6 A.M. to 10 A.M. in other village. It is interesting to note that by 9 A.M. only 50 percent of the households complete their cooking in the canal irrigated village but in contrast almost 100 percent completed their morning cooking is compted in rain-fed village. The observation of the researcher for the variation in the cooking timing of the sample households in these two sample villages is influenced by the occupational structure of the members of the households. The occupation structure which is dominated by casual work in rain-fed village has an influence on the timing of morning cooking as they have to reach the work site before 9 A.M.

Table 1
Distribution of the Households According to the Timing of Morning Cooking

Canal Irrigated Village				*Rain-fed Village*			
Time (A.M.)	*No. of House-holds*	*Percent*	*Cumu-lative Percent*	*Time (A.M)*	*No. of House-holds*	*Percent*	*Cumu-lative Percent*
6	1	0.49	0.49	6	3	2.42	2.42
7	17	8.33	8.82	6.3	2	1.61	4.03
8	27	13.24	22.06	7	71	57.26	61.29
9	67	32.84	54.90	7.3	12	9.68	70.97
10	60	29.41	84.31	8	26	20.97	91.94
11	29	14.22	98.53	8.3	3	2.42	94.35
11.5	2	0.98	99.51	9	5	4.03	98.39
12	1	0.49	100.00	10	2	1.61	100.00
Total	204	100.00	100.00	Total	124	100.00	100.00

The similar type of variations could be observed in the evening cooking timings (Table 2). The evening cooking was completed by 7.30 P.M. by almost all the households in the rain-fed village whereas around 86 percent of the households in canal irrigated village complete their cooking by that time. Therefore, the timing of preparation of the food is influenced by the occupational structure of the households.

Table 2
Distribution of the Households According to the Timing of Evening Cooking

Canal Irrigated Village				*Rain-fed Village*			
Time (P.M)	*No. of House-holds*	*Percent*	*Cumu-lative Percent*	*Time (P.M)*	*No. of House-holds*	*Percent*	*Cumu-lative Percent*
5	1	0.49	0.49	5	16	12.90	12.90
6	8	3.92	4.41	5.3	2	1.61	14.52
7	150	73.53	77.94	6	60	48.39	62.90
7.3	17	8.33	86.27	6.3	10	8.06	70.97
8	24	11.76	98.04	7	31	25.00	95.97
9	4	1.96	100.00	7.3	4	3.23	99.19
Total	204	100.00	100.00	8	1	0.81	100.00
				Total	124	100.00	

Table 3
Food Items Prepared in the Morning and Evening Cooking

(No of Households)

	Canal Irrigated		*Rain-fed*	
Item	*Morning Cooking*	*Evening Cooking*	*Morning Cooking*	*Evening Cooking*
Rice	204	191	124	124
	(100.00)	(93.63)	(100.00)	(100.00)
Sambar	25	20	3	2
	(12.25)	(9.80)	(2.42)	(1.61)
Vegetable Curry	129	95	102	50
	(63.24)	(46.57)	(82.26)	(40.32)
Rasam	74	95	120	120
	(36.27)	(46.57)	(96.77)	(96.770
Vegetables	22	17	12	1
	(10.78)	(8.33)	(9.68)	(0.81)
Dal	37	25	41	31
	(18.14)	(12.25)	(33.06)	(25.00)
Egg	8	13	3	33
	(3.92)	(6.37)	(2.42)	(26.61)
Fish	9	8	2	12
	(4.41)	(3.92)	(1.61)	(9.68)
Chicken	1	5	1	15
	(0.49)	(2.45)	(0.81)	(12.10)
Mutton	2	6	2	4
	(0.98)	(2.94)	(1.61)	(3.23)
Prawn	9	20	2	-
	(4.41)	(9.80)	(1.61)	
Pickel and Papad	13	21	4	6
	(6.37)	(10.29)	(3.23)	(4.84)
Idly with Chutney@	10	14	3	1
	(4.9)	(6.86)	(2.42)	(2.42)
Roti@	15	15	2	3
	(7.35)	(7.35)	(1.61)	(2.42)
Dosa@	9	1	3	1
	(4.41)	(0.49)	(2.42)	(2.42)
Upma@	10	5	6	1
	(4.9)	(2.45)	(4.84)	(2.42)

@ all these are food items prepared with the floors of rice, wheat and black gram etc. Generally they are consumed as items of break fast and alternatives to rice at the dinner

Table 3 presents the food items prepared in the morning and evening cooking. Variations in the food items prepared could be observed from Table 3. Rice is the common food item taken by the sample households in both the villages and almost in the evening and morning. In the canal irrigated village a slight less percentage of households ie., 6.37 are not preparing rice as the main food item in their meal. 'Sambar'[1] is the next item which is generally prepared in the canal irrigated village where as Rasam is the common item preferred by the rain-fed village households. The food habits of the population are generally adopted by the households which are traditionally habituated from their forefathers. The influence of the local availability of food items could be observed in the items they prepared. Prawn is locally available in canal irrigated village due to the presence of inland fish and prawn cultivation in East Godavari District. But consumption of prawn is not seen in rain-fed village as it is not locally available.

Table 4
Sources of Various Food Items

(No. of HH.)

Item	*Canal Irrigated N=204*		*Rain-fed N-124*	
	Home Grown	*Purchased*	*Home Grown*	*Purchased*
Rice	49 (22.00)	155 (76.0)	56 (45.2)	68 (54.8)
Wheat	-	50 (25.00)	-	10 (7.5)
Pulses	3 (1.5)	100 (50.00)	3 (2.4)	20 (16.1)
Milk	4 (2.0)	50 (25.0)	13 (10.5)	62 (50.0)
Oil	2 (1.0)	203 (99.5)	2 (1.6)	122 (98.4)
Eggs	1 (0.5)	36 (17.6)	-	36 (29.0)
Fish	-	31 (15.2)	-	4 (3.2)
Chicken	1 (0.5)	10 (5.0)	9 (7.3)	13 (10.5)
Mutton	-	5 (2.5)	-	4 (3.2)
Vegetables	4 (2.0)	200 (98.0)	4 (3.2)	120 (96.8)
Other food items	-	204 (100.00)	-	204 (100.00)
Tea/Coffee (Preparation)	44 (21.6)	133 (65.2)	20 (16.1)	60 (50.0)

Sources of food items as home grown or purchased throws some light on the existing differences between the two sample villages. In the rain-fed village main item rice is consumed from home grown sources compared to the canal irrigated village. Similarly consumption of milk and chicken is high from home grown sources in rain-fed village than in the canal irrigated village signifies the off farm activities taken by the household members as an alternative source of earnings. More percentage of households have the habit of preparing the tea/ coffee in the house in canal irrigated village than in rain-fed village.

INTRA-HOUSEHOLD DIFFERENCES IN THE FOOD INTAKE

The data on meal pattern of the sample households shows that major percentage in both the categories were following three meals a day (Table 5). But most of the household members consume 'Frigid food'[2] along with raw vegetable like onion or freshly prepared vegetable curry or pickle in the morning. The usual habit of the sample household members is three meals per day either in the form of meals or tiffins. The habit of taking rice three times in a day is high in rain-fed village as it is evident from the percentage i.e., 69.00. In the similar manner having tiffins in breakfast is well in practice in canal irrigated village.

Table 5
Meal/food Pattern Followed by the Members of the Sample Households

Item	*Canal Irrigated Village (Total family members=849)*	*Rain-fed Village (Total family members=616)*
Break Fast+Lunch+Dinner	310 (36.5)	70 (11.3)
Three times Rice	423 (49.8)	425 (69.0)
Lunch+Dinner only	64 (7.5)	59 (9.58)
Lunch+evening Tiffin	52 (6.1)	62 (10.06)

Table 6
Taking Coffee/Tea as a Habit Among the Members of the Sample Households

Item	*Canal Irrigated Village (Total family members=849)*	*Rain-fed Village (Total family members=616)*
Morning Tea/Coffee	191 (22.5)	124 (20.1)
Evening Tea/Coffee	424 (50)	475 (72.1)

From Table 6 it could be observed that the habit of taking evening tea is high among the household members of rain-fed village.

Gender Differences with respect to Meal Pattern

Gender-wise meals pattern of the members of the sample villages is presented in Table 7. Data on meal pattern of the both the genders show that major percentage in both genders are following three meals a day. It could be observed that in canal irrigated village the percentage of household members who are having rice three times per day is around 57–58 percent where as in rain-fed village they constitute nearly 94–96 percent. The major difference in these two villages stems from the nature of work of the household members. In rain-fed village majority of the household members engaged in casual work in which case they generally leave the house by 8.A.M. and return from the work by 6. P.M. They prefer to have rice in their morning first meal rather than having tiffins as breakfast. The percentage of persons who are having food only two times per day is in between 4–5 percent. In canal irrigated areas the percentage of females is higher than that for the males in this category where as the percentage of males is higher in rain-fed village. But on the whole gender differences in the meal pattern could be more in canal irrigated village than rain-fed village. This may be due to the working status of the household members. In canal irrigated village female non-workers are more i.e., 74.9 per cent than in rain-fed village i.e., 66.9 per cent. Therefore, it could be inferred that the working status and the nature of work of individuals will have an influence on the meal pattern of the individual.

Table 7
Meal/food Pattern Followed by the Member of the Sample Households

	Canal Irrigated Village		*Rain-fed Village*	
Item	*Male(N=451)*	*Female (N=398)*	*Male (N=310)*	*Female (N=306)*
Break Fast + Lunch+Dinner	172 (38.14)	143 (35.93)	1 (0.32)	1 (0.33)
Three times Rice	261 (57.87)	234 (58.79)	294 (94.84)	294 (96.08)
Lunch+Dinner only	15 (3.33)	18 (4.52)	14 (4.52)	11 (3.59)
Lunch+evening Tiffen	3 (0.67)	3 (0.75)	1 (0.32)	0 (0.00)

Age Differences with respect to Meal Pattern

The age-wise meals pattern of the members of the sample villages is presented in Table 8.

In the canal irrigated village taking some tiffin in the break fast is the common practice and it is more in children, below 35 years old and above 55 years persons. Taking only two times rice could also be found in all age groups, where as taking rice only ate in the night tiffin is more in the aged people i.e., above 55 years.

In the rainfed village among all the age groups taking rice thrice is common. Taking tiffin in break fast could be found rarely. But taking only 2 times rice item could also be found in the age groups below 55 years in this village.

Therefore, it could be said that the meals patterns of the households is not generally influenced by the age or gender but mostly influenced by the working status and nature of the activity.

INEQUALITIES IN THE CONSUMPTION OF VARIOUS FOOD ITEMS: CANAL IRRIGATED VILLAGE

The computed values of Mean, Standard Deviation, Coefficient of Variation and skewness of various food items for the canal

Table 8
Meal/food Pattern Followed by the Member of the Sample Households

Village	*Canal Irrigated Village (Total family members=849)*					*Rain-fed Village (Total family members=616)*				
Items/ Age groups	*< = 35*	*36-45*	*46-55*	*56-65*	*> = 66*	*< = 35*	*36-45*	*46-55*	*56-65*	*> = 66*
Break Fast+Lunch+Dinner	241	33	45	24	9	0	1	0	2	1
	(42.88)	(25.78)	(45.00)	(54.55)	(60.00)	(0.00)	(0.89)	(0.00)	(4.65)	(5.88)
3 Times Rice	293	92	51	18	4	346	107	79	40	16
	(52.14)	(71.88)	(51.00)	(40.91)	(26.67)	(96.11)	(95.54)	(94.05)	(93.02)	(94.12)
Lunch+Dinner	23	3	4	1	0	13	4	5	0	0
	(4.09)	(2.34)	(4.00)	(2.27)		(3.61)	(3.57)	(5.95)		
Lunch+evening Tiffen	5	0	0	1	2	1	0	0	1	0
	(0.89)			(2.27)	(13.33)	(0.28)			(2.33)	
All	562	128	100	44	15	360	112	84	43	17
	(100.00)	(100.00)	(100.00)	(100.00)	(100.00)	(100.00)	(100.00)	(100.00)	(100.00)	(100.00)

irrigated village are presented in Table 9. The coefficient of variation is very high for all the items except cereals. The skewness is significantly different from zero in all cases which indicates asymmetric consumption of various food items among the households in the sample canal irrigated village. The Histograms with the superimposed normal curves presented in Figure 2 provides visual help in understanding the normality of the consumption of various food items.

Table 9
Inequalities in the Per Capita Consumption of the Various Food Items: Canal Irrigated

Item	*Mean*	*Std. Deviation*	*Coefficient of Variation*	*Skewness*
Cereals	0.4522	0.12982	28.71	2.838
Pulses	0.0207	0.03556	171.79	2.426
Milk	0.1112	0.13739	123.55	2.149
Oil	0.0236	0.01255	53.18	1.684
Eggs	0.1581	0.34561	218.60	1.835
Fish/Chicken/Meat	0.0246	0.12926	525.45	12.913
Vegitables	0.1511	0.10259	67.90	1.470
Other Food Itms	49.3681	22.68013	45.94	1.960

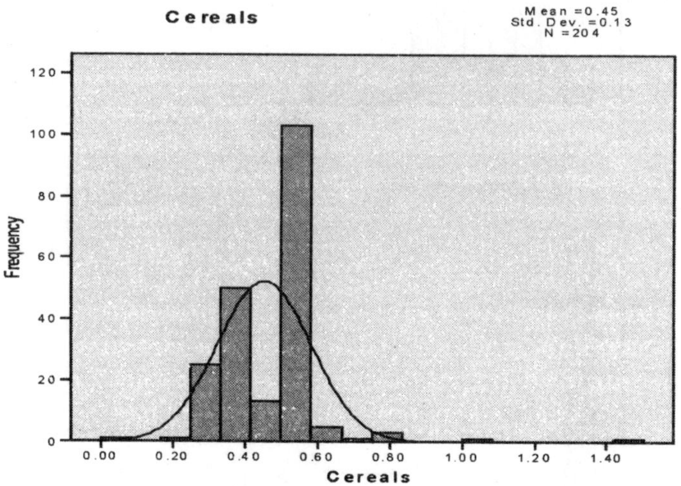

Figure 1: Histograms of Consumption of Various Food Items–Canal Irrigated Village

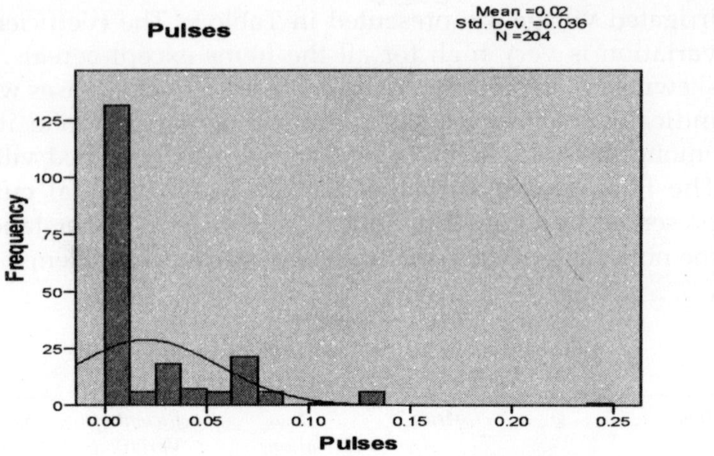
Pulses
Mean =0.02
Std. Dev. =0.036
N =204
Frequency
125
100
75
50
25
0
0.00
0.05
0.10
0.15
0.20
0.25
Pulses

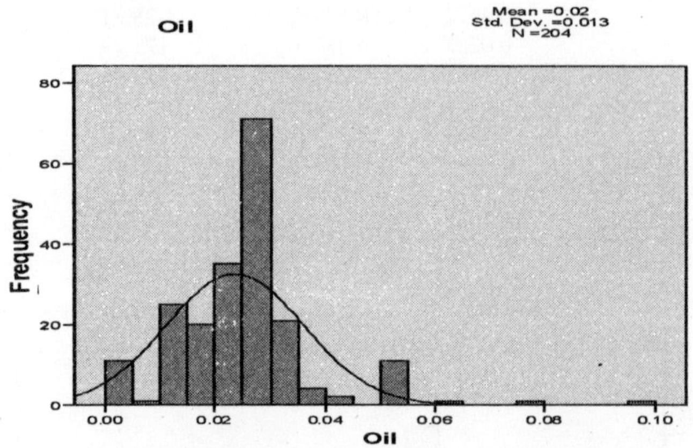
Oil
Mean =0.02
Std. Dev. =0.013
N =204
Frequency
80
60
40
20
0
0.00
0.02
0.04
0.06
0.08
0.10
Oil

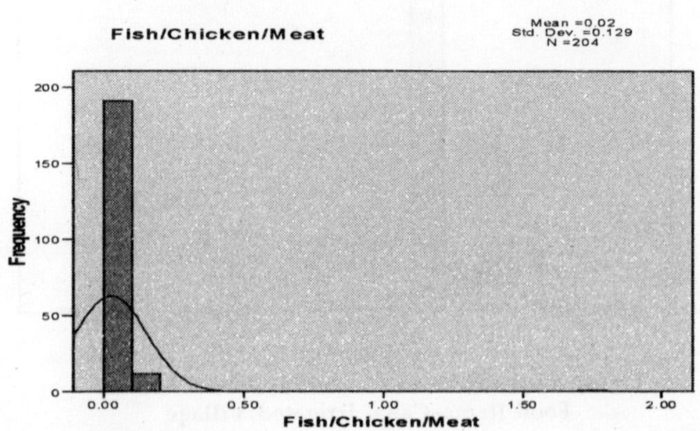
Fish/Chicken/Meat
Mean =0.02
Std. Dev. =0.129
N =204
Frequency
200
150
100
50
0
0.00
0.50
1.00
1.50
2.00
Fish/Chicken/Meat

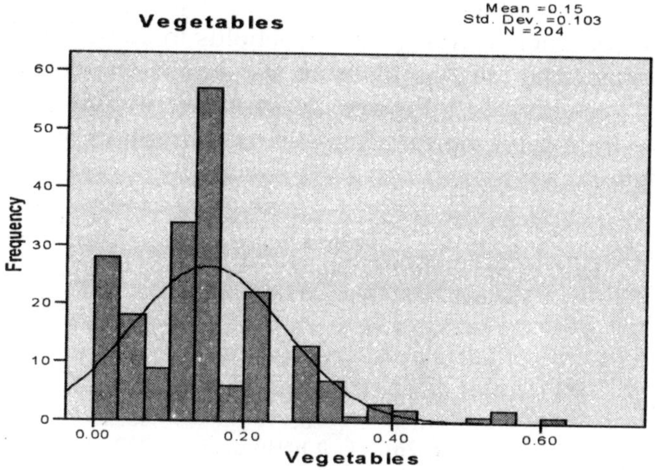

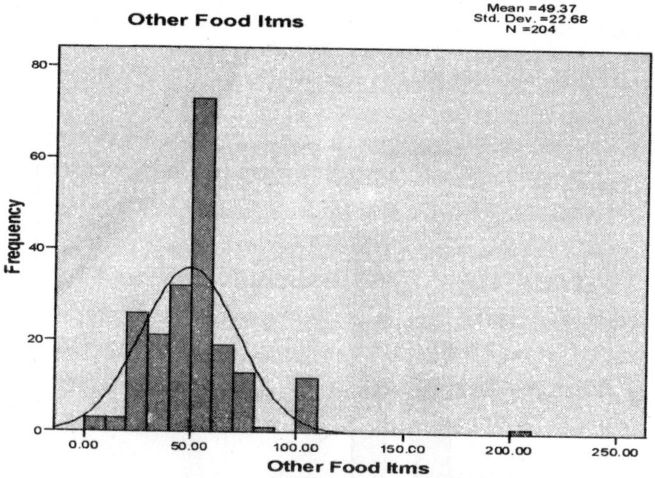

INEQUALITIES IN THE CONSUMPTION OF VARIOUS FOOD ITEMS: RAIN-FED VILLAGE

The computed values of Mean, Standard Deviation, Coefficient of Variation and skewness of various food items for the rain-fed village are presented in Table 10. The Coefficient of Variation is very high for all the items except cereals. The skewness is also significantly different from zero in all cases except cereals which indicates asymmetric consumption of various food items among the households in the sample rain-fed village. The Histograms with the superimposed normal curve presented in Figure 2 provides visual help in understanding the normality of the consumption of various food items.

Table 10
Inequalities in the Per Capita Consumption of the Various Food Items: Rain-fed Village

Food Item	*Mean*	*Std. Deviation*	*Coefficient of Variation*	*Skewness*
Cereals	0.4815	0.13527	28.09	0.968
Pulses	0.0173	0.02714	156.88	1.646
Milk	0.0976	0.10949	112.18	1.498
Oil	0.0323	0.02587	80.09	2.767
Eggs	0.2675	0.45137	168.74	1.389
Fish/Chicken/Meat	0.0214	0.04589	214.44	2.410
Vegitables	0.1476	0.07709	52.23	1.111
Other Food items	35.9022	23.66053	65.90	2.460

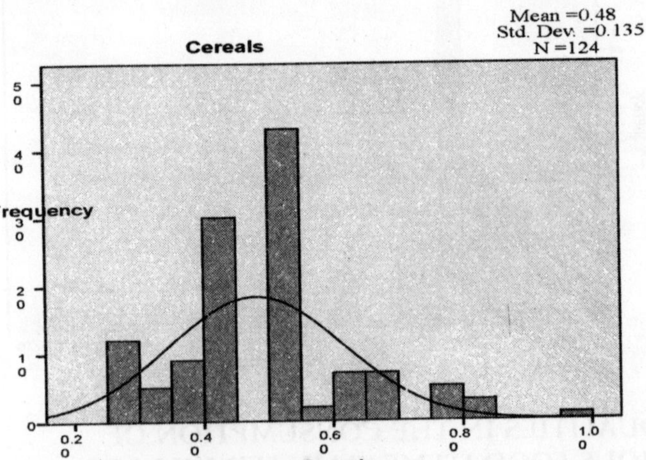

Figure 2: Histograms of Consumption of Various Food Items–Rain-fed Village

SUMMARY

The meal pattern and food items taken are generally influenced by the nature of the activity of the people. Children and the

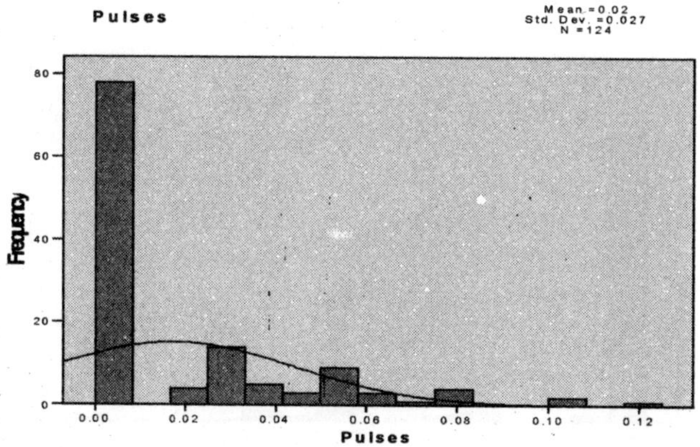
Pulses
Mean =0.02
Std. Dev. =0.027
N =124
Frequency
0
20
40
60
80
0.00
0.02
0.04
0.06
0.08
0.10
0.12
Pulses

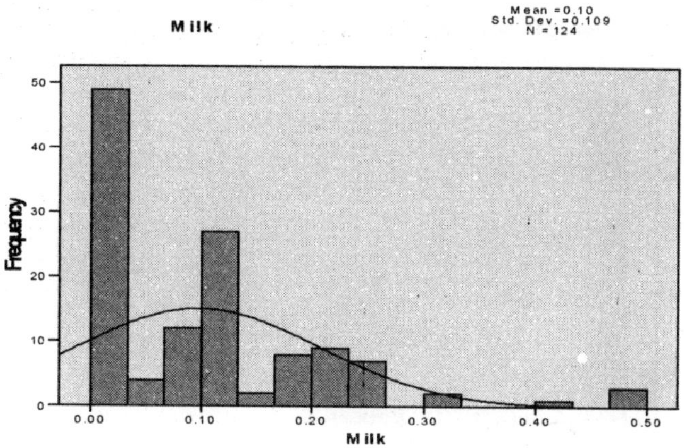
Milk
Mean =0.10
Std. Dev. =0.109
N = 124
Frequency
0
10
20
30
40
50
0.00
0.10
0.20
0.30
0.40
0.50
Milk

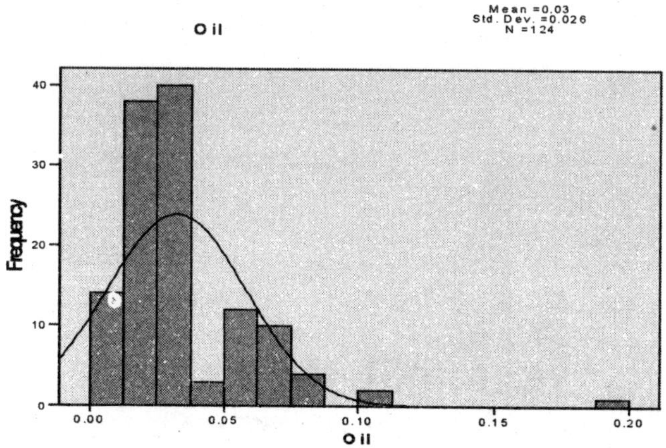
Oil
Mean =0.03
Std. Dev. =0.026
N =124
Frequency
0
10
20
30
40
0.00
0.05
0.10
0.15
0.20
Oil

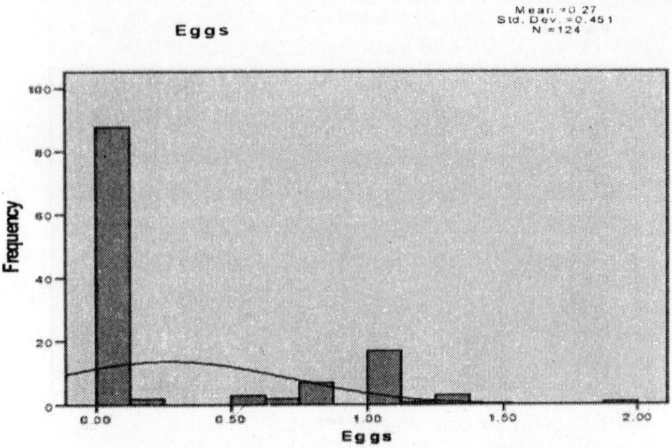
Eggs
Mean =0.27
Std. Dev. =0.451
N =124
Frequency
100
80
60
40
20
0
0.00
0.50
1.00
1.50
2.00
Eggs

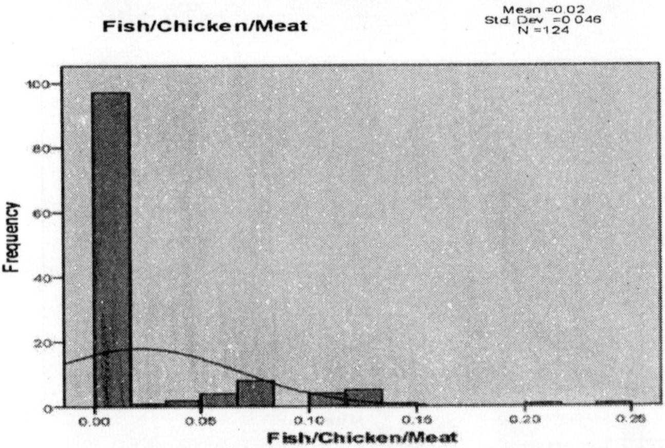
Fish/Chicken/Meat
Mean =0.02
Std. Dev. =0.046
N =124
Frequency
100
80
60
40
20
0
0.00
0.05
0.10
0.15
0.20
0.25
Fish/Chicken/Meat

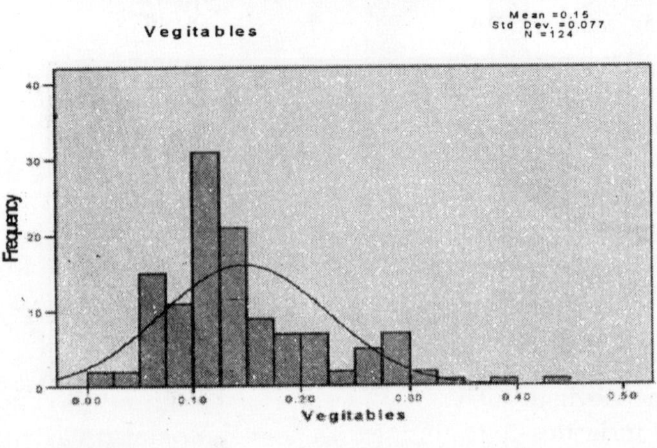
Vegitables
Mean =0.15
Std. Dev. =0.077
N =124
Frequency
40
30
20
10
0
0.00
0.10
0.20
0.30
0.40
0.50
Vegitables

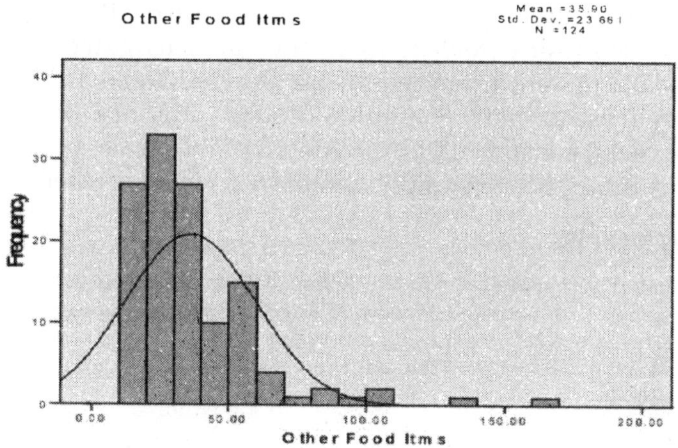

aged take tiffins like idly, dosa, rawa upma in their first meal. Generally the young and middle aged take rice and vegetable curry in their first meal. With respect to the second meal there exist no differences. But the third meal has difference and generally the quantity of rice is less consumed in third meal. All the food items are prepared by the household itself. Some items like papads and to some extent pickles are purchased from outside. There exist differences in the food items prepared in the two villages. The rice consumption is less during evening in case of the households of canal irrigated village (100% in the morning and 93.63% in the evening).The item known as 'Sambar' is consumed along with the item 'Rasam' in canal irrigated village. Where as 'Rasam' is the compulsory item in the diet of the rain-fed village and hardly the item of 'Sambar' is consumed. 'Dal' combined with leafy vegetables or vegetables is more consumed in rain-fed (33 percent of households) where as only 18 percent of households in canal irrigated village. Generally, non-vegetarian items are consumed more during the evening meal than in the day-time meal in both the villages. Eggs are consumed more in rain-fed village than in canal irrigated village. Prawn consumption is more in canal irrigated village as it is available locally. The asymmetric distribution of consumption of various food items clearly indicates that among the households also variations exist as they are dependent on different factors. But only the consumption of cereal items in the canal irrigated village turned out to some extent symmetric. As East Godavari District is known as rice bowl of Andhra Pradesh and 'rice' being the major cereal consumed, the influenced of the locally produced food grain in the consumption pattern is clearly evident.

FOOTNOTES

1. 'Sambar' is prepared by combining 'Dal' with tamarind juice. 'Rasam' is prepared with tamarind juice by adding some specified spice powder.
2. The rice cooked during the evening was placed in the liquid starch added with salt. It was believed that this process will add nutritional values for the food.

6

NUTRITIONAL STATUS OF THE SAMPLE HOUSEHOLDS

INTRODUCTION

According to a survey in 1997 by NSSO, only 10.40 per cent of households in rural Orissa consumed less than 1890 kcal (per cu/day), the cut-off used to determine the extent of absolute hunger[1]. While this may be taken to mean that Orissa has fared relatively better in respect of 'calorie poverty' as compared to 'income poverty', certain limitations of the calorie intake approach to measure undernutrition should be noted[2]. First, the data on calorie intake is typically for a given reference period (of 7 or 30 days). Thus, the short-term variations in food consumptions are not captured by this method of data collection. In addition, variations in the average calorie requirement of a person due to factors like body weight, nature of work performed and status of health are not taken into account. This makes it difficult to have a single required norm of calorie intake below which an individual may be considered undernourished. Second, the calorie intake approach tends to overestimate average calorie intake as it takes into account the total quantity of food consumed by a household during the reference period rather than the normal level of food consumption. Third, and perhaps the most relevant in the present context is that a high level of calorie intake does not necessarily ensure satisfactory nutritional status since efficient absorption of food depends on a number of health related factors like living conditions of a household, state of hygiene and sanitation, and access to safe drinking water. Therefore, anthropometric indicators have a distinct advantage, in terms of validity and reliability, over the calorie intake approach in measuring and monitoring nutritional status.

All these arguments on the measurement issue are subjected to the willingness and response of the respondents in providing information during the time of investigation. Not only that, generally in rural areas they are not aware of their heights and weights. Not even they are sure of exactly remembering their age. Rural people particularly females are hesitant to discuss the information needed for anthropometric indicators. Therefore the present study follows the measure of assessing the nutritional status on the calorie intake method. One comparative study conducted in Maharashtra and Andhra Pradesh villages estimated that considerable under nutrition was observed in the sample both with respect to calories and proteins. Calorie under nutrition was more pronounced in case of Maharashtra villages, while protein under nutrition was relatively more in Andhra Pradesh villages[3].

This Chapter is divided into two sections. Section–I presents the differences in intake of calories, protein consumption, consumption of fats among the sample households of the canal irrigated and rain-fed villages. Section–II presents the inequalities in nutrition status among the sample households of the canal irrigated and rain-fed villages. The normal level of calorie intake considered for the Study is 2700 calories per consumer unit per day[4].

SECTION - I

DIFFERENCES IN CALORIE CONSUMPTION

The nature of inequality has been analysed, with the help of intake of calories in terms of per consumer unit per diem. The analysis was carried out according to family size, occupation and caste. The nature of inequality has been assessed by comparing the values of mean. For easy understanding of the inequalities in the intake of calories, graphical presentation was done by using histogram.

Table 1 presents the average calorie intake, protein and fat consumption in rain-fed village compared to canal irrigated village. It could be observed from Table 1 that the average calorie intake is higher in rain-fed village compared to canal irrigated village. The average calorie intake in rain-fed village is higher than the normal level where as it is less than the normal level in canal irrigated village.

Table 1
Per Consumer Unit Per diem Intake of Calories, Proteins and Fats in Canal Irrigated and Rain-fed Villages

Item	*Canal Irrigated*	*Rain-fed*	*Difference in Per Consumer Unit Per Diem Intake of Calories between Canal Irrigated and Rain-fed*
Calories(Kcal)	2677	2850	173
Proteins(gm)	65	65	3
Fats(gm)	45	56	11

Differences in Calorie Consumption: Family Size

Table 2 presents the intake of calories in terms of per consumer unit per diem under three categories of family sizes viz., 1-3, 4-6, and 7 & above.

Table 2
Per Consumer Unit Per diem Intake of Calories in Canal Irrigated and Rain-fed Villages by Family Size

Family Size	*Canal Irrigated*	*Rain-fed*	*Difference in Per Consumer Unit Per Diem Intake of Calories Between Canal Irrigated and Rain-fed*
1-3	3377	3521	144
4-6	2500	2693	193
7 and above	2637	2661	24
Total	2677	2850	173

It could be observed from Table 2 that the average calorie intake is higher among all the family size groups in rain-fed village compared to Canal irrigated village. The family size group of 4-6 has difference followed by the size group of 1-3 members. It is interesting to observe that except the size group of 1-3 the other groups are having lower average calorie intake than the normal level of calorie intake.

Differences in Calorie Consumption: Occupation

Table 3 presents the intake of calories in terms of per consumer unit per diem under various occupational categories of sample households viz., Cultivator, Agricultural Labour, Casual Worker, Services, Business, and Employed.

Table 3
Per Consumer Unit Per diem Intake of Calories in Canal Irrigated and Rain-fed Villages by Occupation

Occupation	*Canal Irrigated (K.Cal)*	*Rain-fed (K.Cal)*	*Per Consumer Unit Per Diem Intake of Calories between Difference in Canal Irrigated over Rain-fed Village*
Cultivator	2934	3227	293
Agricultural labour	2503	2768	265
Services	2653	2715	62
Business	2757	2513	244
Employed	2538	2663	125
Total	2677	2850	173

It could be observed that the average calorie intake is higher among all the occupational groups in rain-fed village compared to canal irrigated village. The cultivator group has the highest difference followed by the business group. It is interesting to observe that in both the villages, level of calorie intake of cultivator group has been higher than the normal level. Where as agricultural labour and service persons in rain-fed village and business people in canal irrigated village have calorie intake more than normal level. The margin is very less.

Differences in Calorie Consumption: Caste

Table 4 presents the intake of calories in terms of per Consumer unit per diem under different castes of sample households viz.,

Kapu, KoppulaVelama, VishwaBrahmin, Rajak, Madiga, Mala, and others.

Table 4
Per Consumer Unit Per diem Intake of Calories in Canal Irrigated and Rain-fed Villages by Caste

Caste	*Canal Irrigated (K.Cal)*	*Rain-fed (K.Cal)*	*Per Consumer Unit Per Diem Intake of Calories between Difference in Canal Irrigated over rain-fedVillage*
Kapu	2668	-	-
KoppulaVelama	-	2997	-
ViswaBrahmin	3010	2553	457
Rajak	2676	2971	295
Madiga	2846	2473	373
Mala	2583	-	-
Others	3387	2432	955
Total	2677	2856	173

It could be observed from Table 4 that the canal irrigated village is dominated by the 'kapu' caste and Rain-fed village is dominated by 'Koppala Velama" caste. The average calorie intake of kapu caste of the canal irrigated village is lower than the normal level. The average calorie intake of koppala velama caste of the rain-fed village is higher than the normal level. The influence of the caste on calorie intake can't be clearly inferred from the results.

Differences in Protein Consumption: Family Size

Table 5 presents the protein consumption in terms of per consumer unit per diem under three categories of family sizes viz., 1-3, 4-6, and 7 & above.

Differences in Protein Consumption: Occupation

Table 6 presents protein consumption in terms of per consumer unit per diem under various occupational categories of sample households viz., Cultivator, Agricultural Labour, Casual Worker, Services, Business, and Employed.

Table 5
Per Consumer Unit Per diem Protein Consumption in Canal Irrigated and Rain-fed Villages by Family Size

Family Size	*Canal Irrigated (gms)*	*Rain-fed (gms)*	*Per Consumer Unit Per Diem Protein Consumption Between Difference in Canal Irrigated over Rain-fed Village*
1-3	91	78	13
4-6	58	63	5
7 and above	61	61	0
Total	65	65	0

Table 6
Per Consumer Unit Per diem Protein Consumption in Canal Irrigated and Rain-fed Villages by Occupation

Occupation	*Canal Irrigated (gms)*	*Rain-fed (gms)*	*Per Consumer Unit Per Diem Protein Consumption between Difference in Canal Irrigated over Rain-fed Village*
Cultivator	70	73	3
Agricultural labour	57	61	3
Services	84	63	21
Business	63	60	3
Employed	57	63	6
Total	65	65	0

Differences in Protein Consumption: Caste

Table 7 presents the protein consumption in terms of per consumer unit per diem under different castes of sample households viz., Kapu, KoppulaVelama, VishwaBrahmin, Rajak, Madiga, Mala, and Others.

Differences in Consumption of Fats: Family Size

Table 8 presents the intake of fats in terms of per consumer unit per diem under three categories of family sizes viz., 1-3, 4-6, and 7 & above.

Table 7
Per Consumer Unit Per diem Protein Consumption in Canal Irrigated and Rain-fed Villages by Caste

Caste	*Canal Irrigated (gms)*	*Rain-fed (gms)*	*Per Consumer Unit Per Diem Intake of Calorie Protein Consumption between Difference in Canal Irrigated over Rain-fed Village*
Kapu	62	-	-
KoppulaVelama	-	68	-
ViswaBrahmin	72	56	16
Rajak	86	73	13
Madiga	66	54	12
Mala	60	-	-
Others	68	57	11
Total	65	65	0

Table 8
Per Consumer Unit Per diem Intake of Fats in Canal Irrigated and Rain-fed Villages by Family Size

Family Size	*Canal Irrigated (gms)*	*Rain-fed (gms)*	*Per Consumer Unit Per Diem Intake of Fats between Difference in Canal Irrigated over Rain-fed Village*
1-3	71	73	2
4-6	39	52	13
7 and above	34	49	15
Total	45	56	11

Differences in Consumption of Fats: Occupation

Table 9 presents the intake of fats in terms of per consumer unit per diem under various occupational categories of sample households viz., Cultivator, Agricultural Labour, Casual Worker, Services, Business, and Employed.

Differences in Consumption of Fats: Caste

Table 10 presents the intake of fats in terms of per consumer unit per diem under different castes of sample households viz., Kapu, KoppulaVelama, VishwaBrahmin, Rajak, Madiga, Mala, and others.

Table 9
Per Consumer Unit Per diem Intake of Fats in Canal Irrigated and Rain-fed Villages by Occupation

Occupation	*Canal Irrigated (gms)*	*Rain-fed (gms)*	*Per Consumer Unit Per Diem Intake of Fats between Difference in Canal Irrigated over Rain-fed Village*
Cultivator	52	79	27
Agricultural labour	35	47	12
Services	35	29	6
Business	49	47	2
Employed	66	55	11
Total	45	56	11

Table 10
Per Consumer Unit Per diem Intake of Fats in Canal Irrigated and Rain-fed Villages by Caste

Caste	*Canal Irrigated*	*Rain-fed*	*Per Consumer Unit Per Diem Intake of Fats between Difference in Canal Irrigated over Rain-fed Village*
Kapu	48	-	-
KoppulaVelama	-	65	-
ViswaBrahmin	95	35	60
Rajak	35	34	1
Madiga	32	46	14
Mala	32	-	-
Others	64	39	25
Total	45	56	11

INEQUALITY IN NUTRITION STATUS:

Initially, the percentage of the households who are having less than the normal calorie intake is calculated.

The extent of inequality has been measured with the help of Gini ratios. In order to measure the extent of inequalities in nutritional status or in other words under-nutrition, the formula for Sen's Index of Poverty is converted as Index of under-nutrition U.

The following formula is used:

$$U = q \mid (z - m)(1 - G_{ni}) \mid / z^*n$$

Where

'U' is index of under-nutrition

'q' is number of people below the level of minimum calorie intake

'z' is minimum level of calorie intake

'm' is the mean level of calorie intake

'n' is the total sample population

'G_{ni}' is the Gini Co-efficient of the distribution of calorie intake among the sample population.

Gini Ratios are calculated by using the formula.

$$G = 1 + \frac{1}{n} - \frac{2}{n^2 m} \sum_{i=1}^{n} y_i \, (n + 1 - i)$$

$$Y_1 \leq Y_2 \leq Y_3 \ldots\ldots\ldots\ldots\ldots\ldots \leq Y_q$$

Where

m = Per consumer unit and per diem intake of Calories (kcal)

n = No. of Households

y_i = Actual Intake of Calories of ith household

Table 11
Under Nutrition Index for the Canal Irrigated and Rain-fed Villages

Type of Village	*Percentage of Households below the Normal Level of Calorie Intake*	*Under-nutrition Index*
Canal Irrigated	50.83	0.0037
Rain-fed	48.39	0.0232

The empirical results show (Table 11) that the percentage of households whose calorie intake is less than the normal level of 2700 calories is higher in canal irrigated village (50.83) than rain-fed village (48.39). Under-nutrition Index of calorie intake indicates that the severity of under-nutrition among sample households is high in canal irrigated village than rain-fed irrigated village.

SHARE OF FOOD GROUPS IN CALORIE, PROTEIN AND FAT INTAKE[5]

It could be observed from the Tables 12, 13 and 14 that the highest contribution above 75 percent of calories and proteins is from Food Group I (cereals). The contribution of fats is highest from Food Group VIII. In the calorie intake food group VIII (edible oils and milk products) is contributing more in canal irrigated village than in rain-fed village where as food group IX (oil seeds and spices) is contribution more in than canal irrigated village. For the items under various food groups and their calorie conversion is given by NSSO. (See the Nutrition Chart enclosed at the end). With respect to protein contribution it is once again food group I which contributes more in both the villages. Not much variation could be found with respect to the protein contribution of various food groups in both the villages.

With respect to fats the contribution of food group VIII is the highest among all groups. Variation in both the villages could be observed in both the villages.

SUMMARY

The average calorie intake is higher in rain-fed village compared to canal irrigated village. The average calorie intake in rain-fed village is higher than the normal level where as the calorie intake is less than the normal level in canal irrigated village. The average calorie intake is higher among all the family size groups in rain-fed village compared to canal irrigated village. The family size group of 4-6 has the highest difference followed by the size group of 1-3 members. It interesting is to observe except the size groupof 1-3 the other groups are having lower average calorie intake than the normal level of calorie intake. The average calorie intake is higher among all the occupational groups in rain-fed village compared to canal irrigated village. The average calorie intake is higher among all the occupational groups in rain-fed village

Table 12
Per Consumer Unit Per diem Share of CALORIES from Different Food Groups

(Percent)

Sample Village	*I*	*II*	*III*	*IV*	*V*	*VI*	*VII*	*VIII*	*IX*	*Total*
Canal Irrigated	72.904	1.393	2.238	2.287	0.052	2.094	4.254	12.471	2.297	100
Rainfed	73.195	1.035	2.477	2.886	0.071	1.977	4.962	9.668	3.730	100

Table 13
Per Consumer Unit Per diem Share of PROTEINS from Different Food Groups

(Percent)

Sample Village	*I*	*II*	*III*	*IV*	*V*	*VI*	*VII*	*VIII*	*IX*	*Total*
Canal Irrigated	69.832	1.398	0.025	6.469	2.225	11.597	7.403	-	1.051	100
Rainfed	66.435	1.016	0.026	7.763	2.487	12.467	8.212	-	1.594	100

Table 14
Per Consumer Unit Per diem Share of FATS from Different Food Groups

(Percent)

Sample Village	*I*	*II*	*III*	*IV*	*V*	*VI*	*VII*	*VIII*	*IX*	*Total*
Canal Irrigated	6.317	0.104	0	2.647	2.525	5.175	14.713	68.465	0.053	100
Rainfed	7.457	0.092	0	3.872	3.391	4.121	19.782	61.174	0.112	100

compared to canal irrigated village. The average calorie intake of 'kapu' caste of the canal irrigated village is lower than the normal level. The average calorie intake of 'koppala velama' caste of the rain-fed village is higher than the normal level. The influence of the caste on calorie intake cannot be clearly inferred from the results. The percentage of households who's calorie intake is less than the normal level of 2700 calories is higher in canal irrigated village (50.83) than rain-fed village (48.39). The Under-nutrition Index of calorie intake indicates that the severity of under-nutrition among sample households is high in canal irrigated village (0.0037) than rain-fed irrigated village (0.0232). With respect to the protein consumption no difference exists between the households of the two villages. But differences exist with respect to family size. The family size group of 1-3 consumes more proteins (91 gm in canal irrigated village and 78 gm in rain-fed village) than other two groups. With respect to occupational categories, the service occupational category in canal irrigated village recorded highest grams of proteins (84 gm). Among all the categories cultivators are consuming higher grams of proteins compared to other occupational categories (70 grams in canal irrigated village and 73 grams in rain-fed village). Caste has no significant influence on protein consumption. In case of fat consumption the households of rain-fed village record more grams than the households of canal irrigated village (45 grams in canal irrigated village and 56 grams in rain-fed village). According to the family size analysis the family size 1-3 is consuming more units of fats than other family sizes, almost double in grams. With respect to occupational groups, cultivators and employees recorded higher units of consumption than other occupations. In case of fat consumption also, the caste has not recorded major differences.

FOOTNOTES

1. NSSO (1997)
2. Mishra (2003): pp. 9–10
3. (www.icrisat.org)
4. NSSO: Servekshana, October–December 1997, p.9

7

SUMMARY AND CONCLUSIONS

INTRODUCTION

Generally it is argued that low agricultural production and lack of an appropriate food distribution system are the reasons for low levels of the nutritional status. In addition to the low agricultural production, the low nutritional status of the rural population is to be viewed as the problem of poor quality of food intake due to low literacy and lack of awareness. Food consumption expressed in kilocalories (kcal) per capita per day is a key variable used for measuring and evaluating the evolution of the global and regional food situation. A more appropriate term for this variable would be "national average apparent food consumption". Food security has been a major goal of development policy in India since the beginning of planning.

The achievement of macro food grain security at the national level did not percolate down to households and the level of chronic food insecurity in India still is high. However, while average per capita foodgrain availability nearly corresponds to per capita requirements in view of gross iniquities with regard to food distribution, large proportion of poor households do not have access to adequate food. India's nutrition problem is thus not only lack of adequate supply and access to food, for the nearly 30 percent of poor households whose family incomes are low but also lack of proper dietary practices, even if 70 per cent of that family income is spent on food, nutritional needs are not met.

A substantial amount of empirical work has been done in India on food production, food security, distributional aspects and welfare measures which aim at improving the nutritional status of the people. In the existing literature large amount of effort could be observed on nutritional indicators as per capita income or expenditure and on the extent of inequality and poverty. But not much work has been done on the behaviour of the intake of nutrition. A large number of studies focused on the average intake of calorie and protein and the size distribution of such intake across the population in different states. Inter-state inequality in intake of nutrients has been estimated with the use of available secondary data. Large volumes of literature based on the field survey or primary data are available on nutritional status conducted by nutritional experts in the medicine, anthropologists, nutritional experts are available. But basically these studies take into consideration the anthropometric data to analyse the nutritional status and mal nutrition of the persons. Generally these studies had been carried out for specific groups of population like children, women and for specific regions like tribal population. The studies which assess the influence of the agricultural development on nutritional status of household are scanty. Particularly, the studies based on the primary data are meager. Thus any study which aims at understanding the influence of agricultural development on the nutritional status of the rural people gains importance due to first hand information on household level.

Need for the Study

Promoting healthy diets requires a multi-sectoral approach involving the various relevant sectors in societies. The agriculture and food sector figures must be given due importance in any consideration of the promotion of healthy diets for individuals and population groups. Food strategies must not merely be directed at ensuring food security for all, but must also achieve the consumption of adequate quantities of safe and good quality foods that together make up a healthy diet. Any recommendation to that effect will have implications for all components in the food chain. It is therefore useful at this juncture to examine trends in consumption patterns and deliberate on the potential of the food and agricultural Sector to meet the demands and challenges. Intake of calorie, protein, fat-per diem per consumer unit, distribution of intake of nutrients over different food groups, distribution of households/persons over different calorie intake levels; number of meals taken by households during a day etc., forms the base for nutritional and dietary analysis. The dietary changes that characterize the "nutrition transition" include both quantitative and qualitative changes in the diet. Data on the national availability of the main food commodities provide a valuable insight into diets and their evolution over time. Although such average per capita supplies are derived from national data, they may not correspond to actual per capita availability, which is determined by many other factors such as inequality in access to food. Likewise, these data refer to "average food available for consumption", which, for a number of reasons (for example, waste at the household level), is not equal to average food intake or average food consumption. Actual food availability may vary by region, socioeconomic level and season. Based on national data, such averages do not provide information on the distribution of food within communities and households. Per capita intake of calorie and protein based on the averages does not say much about the real nutritional situation of household. It is more pertinent to ask, who is consuming how much?. This perhaps cannot be answered with the available grouped data. Even if household level data are available this generally ignores intra-household distribution. It is important to examine the extent of inter-household and intra-household inequality in food intake and nutritional status. A substantial amount of empirical work has been done in India on such welfare indicators as per capita income or expenditure and on the extent of inequality and poverty. But not much work has been done on the behaviour of the intake of nutrition. The importance of irrigation in foodgrain production was well recognised and efforts during the past five decades enhanced the irrigation facilities for an appreciable extent. But still difference exit in canal irrigated areas and tank irrigated areas where the availability of water depends on the rainfall. This inturn influences the food consumption patterns of the rural people who generally consume locally available and produced food products. Therefore, there is a need to conduct household level study in order to examine the food consumption difference and nutritional differences among the rural households.

OBJECTIVES

The specific objectives of the Study are

1. To examine the food intake and nutritional status of the rural households of Andhra Pradesh based on the NSSO data.
2. To measure the inter-household and intra-household difference in the food intake and consumption pattern of the canal irrigated and rain-fed agricultural villages.
3. To measure the inter-household and intra-household differences in the nutritional status of the canal irrigated and rain-fed agricultural villages.
4. To suggest the policy measures for the improvement of the food intake, consumption pattern and nutritional status of the rural households.

METHODOLOGY

Three-stage random sampling method has been adopted for the Study. In the first stage, two rural mandals from each district was selected. In the second stage two villages namely Repuru from Kakinada rural mandal of East Godavari District and Gutchimi from Seethanagaram mandal of Vizianagaram District were selected. The selection of the village is based on the source of irrigation for the village. The source of irrigation for Repuru village is Government Canal and the source of irrigation for the Gutchimi village is Tank Irrigation. Initially, a census of all households was carried out for the selected villages during January 2007. Based on the village census data, the sample households for detailed survey were enlarged to make it representative and proportional to the number of households. Total households of the selected villages are 817 and 493 respectively for canal irrigated and rain-fed villages. From the canal irrigated village 204 sample households and from rain-fed village 124 sample households were randomly selected which is 25% of the total households of the villages. The Study is based on both primary and secondary data. The secondary data on nutritional status and food intake relating to Andhra Pradesh were taken from various surveys of National Sample Survey Organisation. Pre-tested, structured questionnaires were administered to collect information on socio-economic factors, sources of food availability, food intake, food preparation and related aspects from the sample households. Data regarding food frequency, and intake were collected with the help of questionnaires and structured interviews. Food consumption patterns were recorded using a 24-hour recall. The primary data collected pertain to the period from April 2007 to May 2007 when the temperatures are high. The concepts used in order to calculate the nutritional issues are followed from NSSO surveys.

Nutritional intake of a sample household has been measured by converting the quantities of the items of food consumed by the household into equivalent amounts of energy, protein and fat. The data are analysed by various statistical tools. The conventional techniques such as percentages, averages and ratios were used to analyse and compare the various sources of food and consumption patterns for the two types of villages. The nature of inequality has been assessed by comparing the values of mean, standard deviation and skewness of various food items. For easy understanding of the inequalities in the energy consumption, graphical presentation was also done by using the histogram.

In order to study the nature and extent of inequality per household per diem calorie, Gini ratios were computed. In order to measure the extent of inequalities in nutritional status or in other words under-nutrition, the formula for Sen's Index of Poverty is converted as Index of under-nutrition U.

The following formula is used:

$$U = q \mid (z - m)(1 - G_{ni}) \mid / z\text{-}n$$

Where

'U' is index of under-nutrition

'q' is number of people below the level of minimum calorie intake

'z' is minimum level of calorie intake

'm' is the mean level of calorie intake

'n' is the total sample population

'G_{ni}' is the Gini Co-efficient of the distribution of calorie intake among the sample population.

Findings: A Secondary Data

1. The selected East Godavari District (Canal Irrigation) is one of the agriculturally potential districts. But over a period of time area under cultivation of paddy are sugarcane, are decreasing. The selected Vizianagaram District is also prominent for agriculture in the costal districts. But 80% of area under cultivation depends on the rain-fed conditions. The literacy rate is higher (65.49) in East Godavari District than on Vizianagaram District (51.7). Cultivators are more than agricultural labourers in the East Godavari District where as they are in equal proportion in Vizianagaram District. Non-workers are more than workers in the East Godavari District where as they are of same proportion inVizianagaram District.
2. The selected village viz., Rapuru in canal irrigated District is under the canal cultivation where the water for irrigation is available throughout the year. The village profile shows that agricultural labourer households are more in the village. In the selected village viz., Gutchimi in rain-fed district, of the total area under cultivation, ¼ is irrigated and ¾ is unirrigated. Village profile shows, cultivator

households are more than non-agricultural households. Agricltual labour households are very less.

3. Consumption of rice in Andhra Pradesh is more than All India where as wheat consumption is lower than All India. Bajra and maize also less consumed in Andhra Pradesh compared to All India. Over the period, consumption of the major cereals declined at both State level and All India level. The consumption of bajra and maize per person has also undergone a noticeable decline in rural areas over the eleven years between 1993-94 and 2004-05.
4. There is shift in food consumption throughout the 1990s from cereals, which are a source of cheap calories, to more expensive calorie sources such as Meat, Fish and Eggs and Fruits/Vegetables, resulted in a decline in calorie intake. The calorie share "Other Cereals", such as barley, maize and tapioca, recorded larger declines in rural areas over this period.
5. Interesting thing to notice is that the decline is more during 50th–55th rounds than during 55th -60th rounds. At both state and national levels the per diem intake of calorie is less than the norm i.e., 2700.
6. The decline in cereal consumption, and an increase in the prevalence of undernourishment over the period, 1987/88–2001/2002 suggests that, a need for a reassessment of the current strategy of directing the TPDS exclusively at households "below the poverty line" (BPL).

Findings: Primary Data

1. Kapu is the dominent in the irrigated village where 71.6 percent of the sample households belongs to this caste. Where as in the rain-fed village Koppula velama is the dominent caste where 66.1 percent of the sample households belongs to this caste.
2. In the canal irrigated village, the highest percentage of sample households are agricultural labourers (34.3 percent) followed by cultivators (29.9 percent). Where as in the rain-fed village the highest percentage is cultivators 30.3 percent

followed by agricultural labourers (20.2 percent). Almost equal shares could be observed with respect to occupations of service, business and employment in both the villages.

3. In canal irrigated village, majority of the heads of households are not pursuing any secondary occupation (88.2 percent) and it signifies the adequacy of the work in the main occupation itself through out the year. Generally there will be no slack season which will effect the earning and opportunities for getting work in this village. In case of rain-fed village nearly half of the heads of the household are pursuing secondary occupation in order to feed their families. It clearly indicates the failure of agriculture sector in providing year long employment to the sample households in rain-fed village. No head of the household is having secondary occupation as agricultural labourer. Cultivation is only secondary occupation for nearly 18 percent of sample households in rain-fed village. Highest percent of households are depending on casual work as secondary occupation.
4. Majority of the population are young i.e., below 46 years of age in canal irrigated village whereas in rain-fed majority are above 45 years of age.
5. Majority of the heads of the households are illiterates in canal irrigated where as majority of the household members are illiterates in rain-fed village.
6. More than 80 percent of the sample households possess white colour ration card. This means that they are poor households. Only less than 20 percent of the households are above the poverty line as they possess the Pink colour ration card.
7. In both the villages, majority of the households possess less than or equal to 3 acres of land. But possession of dry land is more in rain-fed village than the canal irrigated village. Cropping differences exist in rain-fed and canal irrigated villages. Janumu was cultivated by less proportion of the households in canal irrigated village where as it is the prominent crop in the rain-fed village.

8. In the rain-fed village, all the sample households are having electricity for lighting whereas in canal irrigated village still few households depend on kerosene for lighting.
9. In both the villages, majority of the households exclusively depend on firewood for cooking purposes where as the use of LPG for cooking is higher in canal irrigated village.
10. Still some percentage of households in rural areas are not having proper dwellings as is evident from the percentage of households living in thatched houses in both the villages.
11. In both the villages, majority of the households prepare food daily twice a day. Most of the households are preparing before 7 a.m. in the morning and in between 6 and 7 p.m. in the evening. They take food daily three times. In the first meal they prepare only some items and the left over quantity prepared during the evening consumed in the First meal is early in the morning. This is the general food practice followed in rural areas.
12. Children and the old people take tiffin like idly, dosa, rawa upma in their first meal. Generally the young and middle aged people take rice and vegetable curry in their 1st meal. With respect to the second meal there exist no differences. But the third meal has difference and generally the quantity of rice is less consumed in third meal.
13. All the food items are prepared by the household itself. The items like papads and to some extent pickles are purchased from outside. There exist differences in the food items prepared in two villages. The rice consumption is less during evening in canal irrigated village (100% in the morning and 93.63% in the evening). 'Sambar' is consumed along 'Rasam' in canal irrigated village. Where as 'Rasam' is the compulsory item in the diet of the rain-fed village and hardly any 'Sambar' is consumed.
14. 'Dal' combined with leaf vegetables or vegetables is more consumed in rain-fed (33 percent of households) where as only 18 percent of households in canal irrigated village.
15. Generally, non-vegetarian items are consumed more during the evening meal than the day-time meal in both

the villages. Eggs are consumed more in rain-fed village than canal irrigated village. Prawn consumption is more in canal irrigated village. Only 2 households out of 124 households consumed prawn in rain-fed village.

16. The average calorie intake is higher in rain-fed village compared to canal irrigated village. The average calorie intake in rain-fed village is higher than the normal level where as the calorie intake is less than the normal level in canal irrigated village.
17. The average calorie intake is higher among all the family size groups in rain-fed village compared to canal irrigated village. The family size group of 4-6 has highest difference followed by the size group of 1-3 members. It is interesting to observe, except the size group of 1-3 other groups are having lower average calorie intake than the norm .
18. The average calorie intake is higher among all the occupational groups in rain-fed village compared to Canal irrigated village. The average calorie intake is higher among all the occupational groups in rain-fed village compared to canal irrigated village.
19. The average calorie intake of 'kapu' caste of the canal irrigated village is lower than the normal level. The average calorie intake of 'koppala velama' caste of the rain-fed village is higher than the normal level. The influence of the caste on calorie intake can't be clearly inferred from the results.
20. Percentage of households whose per day per consumer unit calorie intake is less the normal level of 2700 calories is higher in canal irrigated village (50.83) than rain-fed village (48.39). Under-nutrition Index of Calorie intake indicates that the severity of under-nutrition among sample households is high in Canal irrigated village (0.0037) than rain-fed irrigated village (0.0232).
21. With respect to the protein consumption no difference exists between the households of the two villages. But differences exist with respect to family size. The family size group of 1-3 consumes more proteins (91 gm in canal

irrigated village and 78 gm in rain-fed village) than other two groups. With respect to occupational categories, the service occupational category in canal irrigated village recorded highest proteins (84 gm). Among all the categories cultivators are consuming higher proteins compared to other occupational categories (70 grams in canal irrigated village and 73 grams in rain-fed village). Caste has no significant influence on protein consumption.

22. In case of fat consumption the households of rain-fed village recorded more than the households of canal irrigated village (45 grams in canal irrigated village and 56 grams in rain-fed village). According to the family size analysis the family size 1-3 is consuming more units of fats than other family sizes, almost double. With respect to occupational groups, cultivators and employees recorded higher consumption than other occupations. In case of fat consumption caste has not recorded major differences.

Policy Implications

The Public Distribution System and Rural Employment Programmes should be strengthened to provide better incomes and to ensure proper food supply to the poor as the study identified low nutritional levels in the selected sample villages where more than 80 percent of the population are poor and having white colour ration card. Programmes like Annapoorna Scheme, Antyodaya Anna Yojana should be strengthened to provide food grains to indigent poor and old people. As it is evident from the Study, regional differences exists in the food habit and food consumption patterns, the regional development programmes should incorporate, strategies to increase consumption of local traditional food (particularly pulses, vegetables and animal source food) as an important component of intervention strategies to improve nutritional status. The intra and inter household differences indicate that Nutritional Education efforts should be made to promote appropriate intra-family distribution of food based on requirements and dietary diversification to achieve a balanced intake of all food.

SELECT BIBLIOGRAPHY

Acharya, S.S.(1989), *Socio-economic Impact of 1987 Drought in Rajasthan,* Department of Agricultural Economics, Rajasthan Agricultural University, Jaipur.

Agarwal, K.N. *et al.* (1991), *Growth Performance of Affluent-Indian Children (Under Fives)* Nutrition Foundation of India (NFI), Scientific Report.

AJCN (1982), Report of Working Group on Fortification of Salt (1982) *Am. J. Clin. Nut.*, 34, 1442.

Bandopadhyay, D. (1989), Poverty Alleviation through Special Employment Programmes in Rural India. In: Islam, R. (ed.) *The Elusive Target: The Evaluation of Target-Group Approaches to Employment Creation in Rural India,* New Delhi: ILO/ARTEP, 79-136.

Bardhan, K. (1987): Women's Work, Welfare and Status. *Economic and Political Weekly,* 20 (50), 2207-2220; 20 (51-2), 2261-69.

Basu, K. (1991), The Elimination of Endemic Poverty in South Asia: Some Policy Options,. In: Dreze, J. and Sen, A. (eds) *The Political Economy of Hunger, Volume HI: Endemic Hunger,* Clarendon Press: Oxford.

Berg, A. (1987), *Malnutrition: What Can be Done? Lessons from World Bank Experience,* Johns Hopkins University Press: Baltimore.

Bhalla, G.S. and Gurmail Singh (2001), Indian Agriculture: Four Decades of Development, Sage Publications, N. Delhi

Bhalla, G.S.(1994), "Policies for FoodSecurity in India", in Bhalla, G.S. (ed.) *Economic Liberalisation and Indian Agriculture,* Institute for Studies in Industrial Development, New Delhi.

Bhatt, E. (1991a), Streamlining PDS: Better Targeting is the Key, *The Economic Times,* New Delhi, September 7 1991.

Bhatt, T. (1991b), Employment Programmes: An Assessment, *The Economic Times*, New Delhi, October 1.1991.

Bidinger, P.D., T.S. Walker, B. Sarkar, A. Ram Murthy and P. Babu (1990), *Economic, Health and Nutritional Consequences of the Mid-1980s Drought on a Tank Irrigated, Deccan Village in South India*, Resource Management Programme, Economics Group, Progress Report 98, ICRISAT, Hyderabad.

Brahmam, G.N.V. *et al.* (1988), Intra Family Distribution of Dietary Energy–An Indian Experience. *Ecology of Food and Nutrition.* Vol. 22.

Bulletin of Food Statistics (1986), Government of India, New Delhi.

Census of India (1991), *Andhra Pradesh Provisional Population Totals, Paper 1, Series 2.*

Census of India (1991), *Tamil Nadu Provisional Population Totals, Paper 1, Series 23.*

Central Statistical Organization (CSO) (1989), *National Accounts Statistics.*

Chidambaram, G. (1989), *TINP: Terminal Evaluation, Volume 1.*

Clark, A.W. (1987), The Social Demography of Excess Female Mortality in India: New Directions. Paper prepared for the BAMENEH/American SSRC Workshop on Excess Female Mortality, Dhaka, January 1987.

Clay, E., Harriss, B., Benson, C. and Gillespie, S. (1988), *Food Strategy in India*, Report for the U.K. Overseas Development Administration.

Cornia, G.A., Jolly, R. and Stewart, F. (eds) (1987), *Adjustment with a Human Face Volume I:* Protecting the Vulnerable and Promoting Growth, Clarendon Press: Oxford.

Das Gupta, M. (1987), The Second Daughter: Sex Differentials in Child Mortality, Nutrition and Health Care in Punjab, North India. Paper prepared for the BAMANEH/American SSRC Workshop on Excess Female Mortality, Dhaka, 1987.

Department of Rural Development, Annual Report, Government of India, New Delhi.

Department of Women & Child Welfare (1991), *Status Reports on* ICDS, Government of India, New Delhi, September 30 1991.

Department of Women & Child Welfare, Ministry of Welfare (undated) *Draft National Nutrition Policy.*

Devadas, R. (1987), *Chief Minister's Nutritious Meal Programme: An Appraisal,* Government of Tamil Nadu, Madras.

FAO/WHO (1973), Energy and Protein Requirements, Report of a Joint FAO/WHO Ad Hoc Expert Committee, March 22 - April 2, 1971, *FAO Nutrition Meetings Report Series No. 522,* Rome, Italy; Geneva, Switzerland.

Ferro-Luzzi, A., James, W.P.T. and Waterlow, J.C. (1988), Definition of Chronic Energy Deficiency in Adults. Report of a Working Party of IDECG. *Eur. J. Clin. Nutr.* 969-981.

Gaiha, R. (1991), Poverty Alleviation Programmes in Rural India: An Assessment, *Development and Change,* 22, 117-154.

George, S., Abel, R. and Miller, B.D. (1992), Female Infanticide in Rural South India, *Economic and Political Weekly,* May 30 1992

George, S., Abel, R. and Miller, B.D. (1992), Female Infanticide in Rural South India, *Economic and Political Weekly,* May 30 1992

Ghosh, A. (1991), Eighth Plan: Challenges and Opportunities - XII,. *Economic and Political Weekly* April 30, p 107.

Ghosh, S. *et al. Longitudinal Study of the Survival and Outcome of a Birth Cohort,* Report of the Research Project 01-6582, NCHS, Maryland, USA.

Gillespie, S., and G. McNeill (1994), *Food Health and Survival in India and Developing Countries,* Oxford University Press.

Gillespie, S.R. (1988), Poverty Alleviation in India, In: Clay *et al.* (1988) *op. cit*

Gillespie, S.R. (1989), *Social and Economic Aspects of Malnutrition and Health Among South Indian Tribals.* PhD thesis, London School of Hygiene and Tropical Medicine, University of London. To be published as "Struggle for Health" by Concept, New Delhi.

Gillespie, S.R. and Mason, J.B. (1991), *Nutrition-Relevant Actions,* ACC/SCN State-of-the-Art Series, Nutrition Policy Discussion Paper No. 10, Geneva.

Gillespie, S.R. and Mason, J.B. (1991), *Nutrition-Relevant Actions: Some Experiences from the Eighties and Lessons for the Nineties,* ACC/SCN State-of-the-Art Series, Nutrition Policy Discussion Paper No. 10, United Nations, Geneva.

Gillespie, S.R., Kevany, J. and Mason, J.B. (1991), *Controlling Iron Deficiency,* ACC/SCN State-of-the-Art Series, Nutrition Policy Discussion Paper No. 9, Geneva.

Gopalan, C. (1995), "Towards Food and Nutritional Security", *Economic and Political Weekly*, Vol. 30, No. 52, December 1995, pp. A-134-141.

Government of Andhra Pradesh (1992), Directorate of Health and Family Welfare

Government of India (1987), Department of Rural Development, *Concurrent Evaluation of IRDP: Main Findings of the Survey for October 1985 to September 1986*, New Delhi.

Government of India (1988), *Seventh Plan: Mid-Term Appraisal Report*, New Delhi.

Government of India (1989), *Annual Plan 1989-90*, Planning Commission, Government of India, New Delhi.

Government of India (GOI) (1975-88), *ICDS Evaluation and Research*, Central Technical Committee.

Government of India (GOI) (1983), *National Health Policy*, Ministry of Health and Family Welfare, New Delhi.

Government of India (GOI) (1987), National Sample Survey Organization (NSSO), 42nd Round, July 1986-June 1987, No. 364, Department of Statistics, p 6.

Government of India (GOI) (1988), *Mid-term Appraisal of the Seventh Five Year Plan (1985-90)*, Planning Commission, Government of India, New Delhi.

Government of India (GOI) (1988), *Seventh Five-Year Plan: Mid-Term Appraisal*

Government of India (GOI) (1989), *Health Information of India*, Ministry of Health and Family Welfare.

Government Of India (GOI) (1991), *Economic Survey 1990-91*, Ministry of Finance.

Government of India (GOI) Ministry of Health and Family Planning, Year Books.

Government of Tamil Nadu (1989), *Terminal Evaluation of the Tamil Nadu Integrated Nutrition Project*, Government of Tamil Nadu, Madras.

Gulati, L. (1978), Profile of Female Agricultural Labourers *Economic and Political Weekly*, 13: p 12.

Gupta, S. (1987), Inter-State Variations in Food Consumption, Nutritional Adequacy & Levels of Poverty, *USAID/India Occasional Paper No. 4*, New Delhi.

Hanumantha Rao, D. and J. Gowrinath Sastry (1979), Growth Pattern of Well-to-do Indian Adolescents and Young Adults. *Ind. J. Med. Res. 66*, pp 950-956.

Hanumantha Rao, D., K. Satyanarayana and J. Gowrinath Sastry (1976), Growth Pattern of Well-to-do Hyderabad Preschool Children. *Ind. J. Med. Res. 64*, pp 629-638.

Harriss, B. (1987), Differential Female Mortality and Health Care in South Asia. Report of a Conference held in Dacca, Bangladesh in January 1987 and organised jointly by the South Asian Committee of the American Social Science Research Council and the Bangladesh Association for Maternal and Neonatal Health.

Harriss, B. (1988), Poverty in India: Micro-Level Evidence, Report from a workshop on Poverty in India held at International Development Centre, Queen Elizabeth House, Oxford, mimeo.

Harriss, B. (1990), The Intrafamily Distribution of Hunger, In: Dreze and Sen (eds) *The Political Economy of Hunger Vol. I: Entitlement and Well-being*, p. 351-424.

Harriss, B. (1991), *Child Nutrition and Poverty in India: Noon Meals in Tamil Nadu*, Concept: New Delhi.

Hazell, P.B.R. and Ramaswamy, C. (1991), *The Green Revolution Reconsidered: The Impact of High-Yielding Rice Varieties in South India*, Johns Hopkins University Press, Baltimore, USA.

Heathcote, R.L. (1973), *Drought Perception in the Environmental Economic and Social Significance of Drought* (Lovett, J.V. ed) Sydney, Australia: Angus and Robertson, pp 17-40.

IIPS (International Institute of Populations Studies) (1995), National Family Health Survey (MCH and Family Planning), India 1992-93. Bombay: IIPS.

Indian Council of Medical Research (ICMR) (1977), *Studies on Preschool Children*. Report of the Working Group of ICMR, New Delhi, Technical Report Series No.26.

Indian Council of Medical Research (ICMR) (1981), *Epidemiological Survey of Endemic Goitre and Endemic Cretinism*, An ICMR Task Force Study.

Indian Council of Medical Research (ICMR) (1986), Studies on Weaning and Supplementary Foods: Report of the Working Party of the ICMR.

Indian Council of Medical Research (ICMR) (1990), *A National Collaborative Study of Identification of High Risk Families, Mothers and Outcome of their Off springs, with particular reference to the problem of maternal nutrition, low birth weight, perinatal and infant morbidity and mortality and rural and urban slum communities*, An ICMR Task Force Study.

Indian Council of Medical Research (ICMR) (1991), *Studies on Preschool Children* Report of the Working Group of ICMR, New Delhi, Technical Report Series No. 26.

International Institute of Population Studies (IIPS) and ORC Macro (2000), *National Family Health Survey (NFHS-2), 1998-99*, Mumbai.

International Monetary Fund (IMF) Financial Statistics Yearbooks, selected years.

Jennings, J., Gillespie, S.R., Mason, J.B., Lotfi, M. and Scialfa, T. (1991), *Managing Successful Nutrition Programmes*, ACC/SCN State-of-the-Art Series, Nutrition Policy Discussion Paper No. 8, United Nations, Geneva.

Jha, S. (1991), Targeting subsidies: What needs to be done, *The Economic Times* New Delhi October 16 1991.

Kakwani N. and Subbarao K. (1990), *Rural Poverty in India: 1973-86*, Working Paper, Policy, Research and External Affairs Division, World Bank, Washington D.C.

Kakwani, N. and Subbarao, K. (1990), Rural Poverty in India, 1973-86. World Bank Working Paper Series 526.

Kakwani, N. and Subbarao, K. (1990b), Rural Poverty and its Alleviation in India, *Economic and Political Weekly*, 31 March 1990.

Karakal, M. and Irudeyarajan, S. (1991), *Economic and Political Weekly*, 23 February 1991.

Khatri, G.R. (1990), National Goitre Control Programme *Proceedings of the Workshop on Iodised Salt* National Institute of Nutrition, Hyderabad November 1-2.

Krishna Rao, Y.V. (ed.) (2000), *New Challenges Facing Indian Agriculture*, Visalaandhra Publishing House, Hyderabad.

Krishnan, P. (1975), Mortality Decline in India 1951-61 - Development vs Public Health Programme, *Social science & Medicine*, 90.

Kulkarni G.A. and Kumar A. (1984), Estimates of the Undernourished Population, From Alternate sources *Sarvekshana*, April 1984, p.3.

Kumar, S. (1978), *Role of Household Economy in Child Nutrition at Low Incomes* Occasional Paper No.95; Dept of Agricultural Economics; Cornell University NY.

Kundu, A. and Sahu, M.K. (1991), Variation in Sex Ratio: Development Implications, *Economic and Political Weekly, October 12,* p2341-2.

Leslie, J. and Paolisso, M. (eds) (1989) *Women, Work and Child Welfare in the Third World,* AAAS Selected Symposia Series 110, Westview Press: Boulder, Colarado.

Lipton, M. (1983), *Poverty, Undernutrition and Hunger,* World Bank Staff Working Paper No 597 Washington DC.

Mahalanobis, D. (2005), *"Micronutrient Malnutrition: Some Public Health Concerns"*, in A.K. Bagchi and Krishna Soman (ed.) *Maladics, Preventives and Curatives, Debates In Public Health in India,* Tulika Books.

Martorell, R., and T.J.Ho (1984), "Malnutrition, Morbidity and Mortality", *Population and Development Review,* A Supplement to Vol. 10, pp. 49-68.

Meenakshi, J.V. (1996), "How Important are Changes in Taste? A State Level Analysis of Food Demand", *Economic and Political Weekly,* Vol. 31, No .50, December 14, pp. 3265-69.

Menon, K. and Vijayaraghavan, K. (1980), Sequelae of Severe Xerophthalmia - A Follow-up Study *Am. J. Clin. Nut., Vol 33,* pp 218-220.

Miller, B. (1981), *Neglect of Female Children in Rural North India* Cornell University Press NY.

Miller, B. (1981), *The Endangered Sex: Neglect of Female Children in Rural North India* Cornell Univ. Press. Ithaca, NY.

Miller, B. (1981), *The Endangered Sex: Neglect of Female Children in Rural North India,* Cornell University Press: Ithaca, New York.

Minhas, B.S. (1991), "On Estimating the Inadequacy of Energy Intakes: Revealed Food Consumption Behaviour Versus Nutritinal Norms (Nuritional Status of Indian People in 1983)", *The Journal of Development Studies,* Vol. 28, No. 1, pp. 1-38.

Minhas, B.S., Jain, I.R., Kansal, S.M. and Saluja, M.R. (1987), On the Choice of Appropriate Consumer Price Indices and Data Sets for estimating the Incidence of Poverty in India, *Indian Economic Review,* Vol 12, pp 19-49.

Ministry of Civil Supplies (1991), Government of Andhra Pradesh (personal communication), December 1991.

Ministry of Health & Family Welfare (undated) *Policy on Management of Vitamin A Deficiency*, Government of India, New Delhi.

Ministry of Health and Family Welfare (1988), *Family Welfare Yearbook 1987-88*, Government of India.

Ministry of Health and Family Welfare (1989), *Report of the Meeting on Prevention and Control of Nutritional Anaemia*, Ministry of Health and Family Welfare, Government of India and UNICEF, New - Delhi, November 1989.

Ministry of Health and Family Welfare and UNICEF (1989), Report of the Meeting on Prevention and Control of Nutritional Anaemia, New Delhi, November 1989.

Mohan N. C. (1991), Adjustment with a human face? *The Economic Times*, New Delhi, August 1 1991.

Mohan, C. N. (1991), Adjustment with a Human Face?, *The Economic Times*, New Delhi, August 1 1991.

Mortorell, R. and T.J.Ho (1984), "Malnutrition, Morbidity and Mortality", *Population and Development Review*, A Supplement to Vol. 10, pp. 49-68.

Naidu, A.N. *et al* (1991), Maternal Body Mass Index and Birth Weight *Nutrition News:* Vol. 12, No 2.

Naidu, A.N. *et al* (1991) Maternal Body Mass Index and Birth Weight, *Nutrition News*, Vol. 12, No. 2.

Naidu, A.N. *et al.* (1983), *Nutritional Status of Indian Adults* (assessed by Body Mass Index), National Institute of Nutrition.

National Institute for Public Cooperation and Child Development (NIPCCD) (1991).

National Institute of Nutrition (1983), Growth of Breast-fed Infants in a Slum Population *Annual Report* pp 153-157.

National Institute of Nutrition (1983), Income and Birth-weight *Annual Report* p 125.

National Institute of Nutrition (1985-86), Maternal Size and Birth Weight of Infants *Annual Report*, p 100.

National Institute of Nutrition (2002), *Diet and Nutritional Status of Rural Population, NNMB Technical Report No.21*, National Institute of Nutrition, Hyderabad.

National Institute of Nutrition (NIN) (1991), *Repeat Survey*, National Nutrition Monitoring Bureau, NIN, Hyderabad, India.

National Institute of Nutrition (NIN) (1991b), Unpublished data from Repeat Survey. National Nutrition Monitoring Bureau. NIN, Hyderabad, India.

National Nutrition Monitoring Bureau (1991), *Report of NNMB Repeat Surveys (1988-90)*, National Institute of Nutrition, Hyderabad.

National Nutrition Monitoring Bureau (1993), *Report of NNMB Repeat Surveys (1991-92)*, National Institute of Nutrition, Hyderabad.

National Nutrition Monitoring Bureau (1999), *Report of Second Repeat Survey, Rural NNMB Technical Report No.18*, National Institute of Nutrition, Hyderabad.

National Nutrition Monitoring Bureau (2000), *Diet and Nutritional Status of Tribal Population, Report of First Repeat Survey NNMB Technical Report No.19*, National Institute of Nutrition, Hyderabad.

National Nutrition Monitoring Bureau (NNMB) (1991), *Report of Repeat Surveys.*

National Nutrition Monitoring Bureau (NNMB), *Annual Reports 1975-91.*

Nutrition Foundation of India (NFI) (1988), *Integrated Child Development Services: A Study of some Aspects of the System.* NFI Scientific Report No. 7, New Delhi 1988.

Pelletier, D.L., E.A. Frongillo, Jr., D.G. Schroeder and J.P Habicht (1995), "The Effects of Malnutrition on Child Mortality in Developing Countries", *Bulletin of the World Health Organisation*, Vol. 73, No. 4, pp. 443-448.

Pryer, J. (1989), When Breadwinners Fall III: Preliminary Findings from a Case Study in Bangladesh, *IDS Bulletin* 20 (2), 49-58.

Pulley, R.V. (1989), *Making the Poor Credit Worthy*, World Bank Discussion Paper, Washington DC.

Punhani, R. and Mahajan, R. (1989), *Research on ICDS: An Overview, Volume I (1975-85)*, National Institute of Public Cooperation and Child Development, New Delhi.

Radhaiah, G., Vijayaraghavan, K. and Rao, N.P. (1985), Evaluation of NREP in Andhra Pradesh, *Journal of Rural Development*, 4 (3) May 1985.

Radhakrishna (1992), "Effects of Growth, Relative Price and Preferences on Food and Nutrition", *Indian Economic Review*, Vol. 27, Special Number, pp. 303-323.

Radhakrishna (2001), "Agricultural Growth, Employment and Poverty: A Policy Perspective", Presidential Address,s 43rd Annual Conference of Indian Society of Labour Economics, December 18-21.

Radhakrishna (2002), "Food and Nutrition Security" in Kirit S. Parikh and R. Radhakrishnas (eds.) India Development Report, 2002, Oxford University Press.

Radhakrishna , R. (1991) , "Food and Nutrition: Challenges for Policy", *Journal of the Indian Society of Agricultural Statistics*, Vol. 43, No. 3, pp. 211-227.

Radhakrishna and C. Ravi (1990), *Food Demand Projections for India*, Centre for Economic and Social Studies, Hyderabad.

Radhakrishna K. Subba Rao, S.Indrakant and C. Ravi (1997), *India's Public Distribution System: A National and International Perspective*, World Bank Discussion Paper No. 380.

Radhakrishna, R. (1992), Trends in Nutrition: Emerging Challenges, and Nutrition: Need for Effective Intervention, Two articles for *The Economic Times of India*, February 10-11 1992

Radhakrishna, R. (1992), Trends in Nutrition: Emerging Challenges; and Nutrition: Need for Effective Intervention, *The Economic Times*, New Delhi, February 10 and 11 1992.

Radhakrishna, R., (2005), "Food and Nutrition Security of the Poor: Emerging Perspectives and Policy Issues, *Economic and Political Weekly*, April 30.

Radhakrishna, R., and C. Ravi (1992), "Effects of Growth, Relative Price and Preference on Food and Nutrition", *Indian Economic Review*, 27 (Special Number), 303-323.

Radhakrishna, R., and C. Ravi (2005), "Emerging Nutritional Trends and Their Implications" in A.K. Bagchi and Krishna Soman (ed) *Maladies, Preventives and Curatives: Debates in Public Health in India*, Tulika Books.

Radhakrishna, R., K. Hanumantha Rao, C. Ravi and B. Sambi Reddy (2004), *Chronic Poverty and Malnutrition in India*, Working paper 11, Chronic Poverty Research Centre, Indian Institute of Public Administration, New Delhi.

Radhakrishna. R. and Indrakant (1987), *Effects of Rice Market Intervention Policies in Andhra Pradesh,* Working Paper No. 15, Centre for Economic and Social Studies (CESS), Hyderabad.

Ramachandran, P. (1989), Nutrition in Pregnancy, *In: Women and Nutrition,* Gopalan, C. and Kaur, S (eds.) Nutrition Foundation of India, Special Publication Series No. 5, p 155.

Ranade, S. (1991), Good Times and Bad Times; Indian Politics and the Poor, Article III, *The Hindu,* December 18 1991.

Rao C.H.H.(2000), "Declining Demand for Foodgrains in Rural India: Census and Implications", Economic and Political Weekly, January 22 ?

Rao P. R., Lakshmi R. R. *et al.* (1988), *Nutritional Content of Community Care Services Delivered Through Health and Non-Health Channels: A Multi-Centric Study,* National Institute of Nutrition, Indian Council of Medical Research, Hyderabad.

Rao V.M. and Jeromi P.D.(2000), "Modernizing Indian Agriculture: Priority Tasks and Critical Policies" Study No.21, Department of Economic Analysis and Policy, Reserve Bank of India, Mumbai.

Rao, C.H.H. (2000), "Declining Demand for Foodgrains in Rural India: Causes and Implications", *Economic and Political Weekly,* January 2.

Rao, C.H.H. and R.Radhakrishna (1997), "National Food Security: A Policy Perspective for India", Plenary paper, 27th *International Conference of Agricultural Economists,* August 10-16, Sacramento, California and published in G.H. Peter and J.V. Braun (ed.) Food *Security, Diversification and Resource Management: Re-focussing the Role of Agriculture,* Ashgate, 1999.

Rao, C.H.H., and R. Radhakrishna (1997), "National Food Security: A Policy Perspective for India" in G.H. Peter and J.V. Braun (eds.) *Food Security, Diversification and Resource Management: Re-focusing the Role of Agriculture,* Ashgate, 1999.

Rao, D.H., and J.G. Sastry (1979), Growth Pattern of Well-to-do Indian Adolescents and Young Adults *Ind. J. Med. Res. 66,* pp 950-956.

Ravi, C. (2000), *Complete Demand Systems, Welfare and Nutrition: An Application to Indian Consumption Data,* Centre for Economic and Social Studies, Hyderabad.

Ravi, C. (2000), *Complete Demand Systems, Welfare and Nutrition: An Analysis of Index Consumption Data,* Centre for Economic and Social Studies, Hyderabad.

Reddy S.S. (1991), *Poverty and Agricultural Growth in Rural Andhra Pradesh: Inter District Analysis,* Centre for Economic and Social Studies, Hyderabad, India.

Reddy, V. (1990), *Energy and Protein Requirements* Paper presented at the regional expert consultation of the Asian network for Food and Nutrition Planning, Bangkok, 24-27th July, p 14.

Reddy, V., Rao, P., Shekar, M. and Gillespie, S.R. (1992), *Nutrition in India, Part I,* ACC/SCN, Geneva.

Registrar General (1991), *Population of India, Census Results and Methodology,* Vital Statistics Division, 52-54.

Registrar General of India (1979-86), *Sample Registration System.*

Registrar General of India (1981), *Census.*

Registrar General of India (1982/1986) *Survey on Causes of Deaths (Rural).* Serial No. 3 No. 19.

Registrar General of India (1984), *Survey on Birth Order Differentials.*

Registrar General of India (1987), *Survey of Causes of Death (Rural).*

Registrar General of India (1989), *Census-1981 Occasional Paper* No. 2.

Registrar General of India (1991), *Census Provisional Population Totals.*

Registrar General of India (1991) *Census.*

Rosenzweig, M. R. and P.T. Schultz (1982), Market Opportunities, Genetic Endowments and Intrafamily Resource Distribution: Child Survival in Rural India. *American Economic Review 72* (4): 803-815.

Sarekshama (April-June 1989), *A Note on Consumer Expenditure Survey 42nd Round (July 86-June 87)* Vol. XII, No. 4.

Sarma, J.S. and Gandhi, V.P. (1990), Production and Consumption of Foodgrains in India: Implications of Accelerated Economic Growth and Poverty Alleviation, *IFPRI Research Report No. 81,* July 1990.

Sarma, K.V.R., *et al.* (1990), *ICDS–An Epidemiological and Qualitative Study,* NIN Scientific Report.

Sarvekshana (1990), Volume 8, No. 4, Issue No 43, April-June 1990

Satyanarayana, K. (1989), Nutritional Status and Productivity, International Dietary Energy Consultancy Group, *Annual Report.*

Satyanarayana, K. *et al.* (1986), Effect of Early Childhood Undernutrition and Child Labour on Growth and Adult Nutritional Status of Rural Indian Boys around Hyderabad. *Human Nutrition: Clinical Nutrition,* 40 C, pp 131-139.

Satyanarayana, K. *et al.* (1991), *Body Mass Index and Mortality Pattern– A 10 year Retrospective Study (communicated).*

Sekler, D. (1982), "Small but Healthy", in Sukhatme, P.V. (ed.).

Shekar M. (1991), *The Tamil Nadu Integrated Nutrition Project: A review of the project with special emphasis on the monitoring and information system,* Cornell Food and Nutrition Policy Programme Working Paper No. 14, Ithaca, New York.

Shekar, M., Prahlad Rao, N. Gillespie, S.R. and Reddy, V. (1992), *Nutrition-Relevant Actions in Two South Indian States, Part II of Nutrition In India,* ACC/SCN, Geneva.

Shrimpton R. (1989), *Community Participation in Food and Nutrition Programmes: An Analysis of Recent Governmental Experiences,* Cornell Food and Nutrition Policy Program, Ithaca, New York.

Srikantia, S.G. (1989), Pattern of Growth and Development of Indian Girls and Body Size of Adult India Women, In: Gopalan, C. and Kaur, S. (eds.) *Women and Nutrition in India,* NFI, Special Publications Series 5.

Subbarao, K. (1989), Improving Nutrition in India: Policies and Programmes and their Impact, World Bank Discussion Paper No. 49

Subbarao, K. (1989), *Improving Nutrition in India: Policies and Programmes and Their Impact,* World Bank Discussion Paper No. 49, Washington DC.

Sukhatme, P.V. (1982), "Poverty and Malnutrition", in Sukhatme, P.V. (ed.), *Newer Concepts in Nutrition and Their Implications for Policy,* Maharashtra Association for the Cultivation of Science, Pune, pp. 11-64.

Sundaram, K. and Tendulkar, S.D. (1985), Anti-Poverty Programmes in India: An Assessment, In: Mukhopadhyay, S. (ed) *The Poor in Asia: Productivity-Raising Programmes and Strategies,* Asian and Pacific Development Centre: Kuala Lumpur.

Suryanarayana, M.H. (1991), Measuring Poverty: An Alternative Approach, *The Economic Times,* October 24 1991.

Tandon, B.N. *et al.* (1983), A Coordinated Approach to Children's Health in India: Progress Report after Five Years (1975-80) *Lancet ii,* 109-11.

Tandon, B.N. *et al.* (1984), Impact of Integrated Child Development Services on Infant Mortality Rate in India, *Lancet ii,* 157.

The Tamil Nadu Corporation For Development of Women Limited (1986), *Women in Tamil Nadu: A Profile.*

The Times of India (1992), *Job Guarantee Scheme in Tamil Nadu,* February 8 1992.

UNDP (1990), *Human Development Report,* Oxford University Press for UNDP.

UNICEF (1990), *Children and Women in India: A Situation Analysis,* UNICEF, New Delhi, India.

UNICEF (1990), *Children and Women in India: A Situation Analysis.* UNICEF, New Delhi, India.

UNICEF (1990), *Children and Women in Tamil Nadu: A Situation Analysis,* UNICEF, Madras, India.

UNICEF (1990), *Strategy for Improved Nutrition of Children and Women in Developing Countries,* Policy Review Paper E/ICEF/1990/1.6, UNICEF, New York; JC 27/UNICEF-WHO/89.4. Review, UNICEF, New York.

Vijayaraghavan, K. and Prahlad Rao, N. (1982), An Evaluation of National Prophylaxis Programme against blindness due to Vitamin A deficiency *Nut. Rep. Int.* 25, pp 431-441.

Walker T.S. and Ryan J.G. (1990), *Village and Household Economics in India's Semi-arid Tropics* Baltimore: The Johns Hopkins.

WHO (1981), Report on the WHO Collaborative Study on Breast Feeding, p. 36, 37.

World Bank (1991), *Gender and Poverty in India* The World Bank, Washington DC.

World Bank (1991), *Gender and Poverty in India,* The World Bank, Washington DC.

APPENDIX

Appendix–1
Mandal Details of East Godavari District

Sl. No.	*Name of the Mandal*	*No. of Revenue Villages*	*No. of Panchayats*
1	Maredumilli	71	12
2	Y. Ramavaram	137	17
3	Addateegala	99	22
4	Rajavommangi	62	19
5	Kotananduru	16	28
6	Tuni	22	20
7	Thondangi	15	19
8	Gollaprolu	12	11
9	Shankhavaram	32	19
10	Prathipadu	40	20
11	Yeleswaram	13	13
12	Gangavaram	60	17
13	Rampachodavaram	77	19
14	Devipatnam	46	14
15	Seethanagram	17	17
16	Korukonda	19	20
17	Gokavaram	15	14
18	Jaggampeta	19	16

Contd.

Sl. No.	*Name of the Mandal*	*No. of Revenue Villages*	*No. of Panchayats*
19	Kirlampudi	17	19
20	Peddapuram	22	23
21	Pithapuram	27	24
22	U.Kotapalli	16	16
23	Kakinada ®	15	20
24	Kakinada (U)	4	0
25	Samalkota	19	18
26	Rangampeta	15	16
27	Gandepalli	13	18
28	Rajanagaram	17	25
29	Rajahmundry Rural	9	10
30	Rajahmundry Urban	1	0
31	Kadiam	7	11
32	Mandapeta	14	12
33	Anaparthi	9	11
34	Biccavole	14	12
35	Pedapudi	17	18
36	Karapa	19	23
37	Tallarevu	13	17
38	Kajuluru	20	26
39	Ramachandrapuram	22	25
40	Rayavaram	10	12
41	Kapileswarapuram	15	19
42	Alamuru	15	18
43	Atreyarapuram	15	17
44	Ravulapelm	11	12
45	Pamarru	24	26

Contd.

Sl. No.	Name of the Mandal	No. of Revenue Villages	No. of Panchayats
46	Kothapeta	10	10
47	P.Gannavaram	18	20
48	Ambajipeta	13	16
49	Ainavilli	17	21
50	Mummidivaram	11	19
51	I. Polavaram	11	14
52	Katrenikona	14	16
53	Uppalaguptam	14	17
54	Amalapuram	17	22
55	Allavaram	14	21
56	Mamidikuduru	17	18
57	Razole	13	16
58	Malkipuram	11	20
59	Sakhinetipalli	8	16
60	Rowthulapudi	44	0

Appendix–2
Mandal Details of Vizianagaram District

S. No.	*Name of the Mandal*	*No of Revenue Villages*	*No of Panchayats*
1	Vizianagaram	23	21
2	Gantyada	45	35
3	Bhogapuram	22	22
4	Denkada	28	26
5	Pusapatirega	37	27
6	S.Kota	40	26
7	Jami	28	25
8	Kothavalasa	28	25
9	Vepada	39	29
10	L.Kota	32	31
11	Nellimarla	33	28
12	Gurla	39	37
13	Cheepurupalli	32	17
14	Garividi	38	28
15	Merakamudidam	41	24
16	Gajapathinagaram	35	28
17	Bondapalli	33	26
18	Dattirajeru	46	35
19	Mentada	37	30
20	Parvathipuram	54	26
21	Komarada	99	31

Contd.

S. No.	*Name of the Mandal*	*No of Revenue Villages*	*No of Panchayats*
22	Garugubilli	34	28
23	Jiyyammavalasa	58	31
24	Kurupam	95	23
25	Gummalaxmipuram	124	27
26	Badangi	29	25
27	Therlam	50	32
28	Saluru	90	29
29	Pachipenta	54	28
30	Makkuva	54	21
31	Ramabhadrapuram	32	22
32	Bobbili	44	30
33	Seethanagaram	44	34
34	Baligipeta	34	24
	Total	1551	931

Appendix–3
Calorie Norm

Pegging the level of the calorie norm has long been subject to debate and many norms are in use. The following are the few words on the various norms in use. The average calorie norm of 2100 calories per capita per day prescribed by the FAO for South Asia[1] is far lower than the 2400 calories that is conventionally adopted in India for nutritional analysis in rural areas. The FAO also uses a different cut-off of 1810 calories for India to represent the lower-end range of food requirements[2]. In fact the difference is explained by the fact that the 2400 figure represents an 'average' requirement, incorporating a margin of 'safety', while the 1810 figure represents a 'minium' amount necessary for good health. Researchers like P V Sukhatma argue against the use of any norm for measuring the deprivation. He suggested that the body's adaptation mechanisms enable those with lower body weights to metabolise a lower amount of calories more efficiently, invalidating the use of a biologically-derived nutrient norm[3]. Although the problem of the 'troublesome norm' is certainly not a new one, the debate has by and large been inconclusive. It is perhaps also useful to reiterate a point that may seem obvious: nutritional requirements vary not only with climate, but also with gender, age and activity status. In fact, 2400 calories corresponds to the National Institute of Nutrition's Recommended Daily Allowance (RDA) for an adult male weighing 60kg, engaged in sedentary work. The RDA for an adult woman also engaged in sedentary activity is 1875 calories per day. The corresponding recommendations for moderate work are 2875 and 2225 calories respectively, while those for children below 18 are much lower[44]. One method of incorporating these differing needs is to define the norm in terms of consumer units. An adult male is taken as the reference individual (unity), and age and gender-specific conversion factors (less than unity) are then applied to other members of the household to obtain the total number of consumer units per household. The corresponding norm has been determined as 2700 calories per consumer unit per day. This study uses this concept of per consumer unit per day unit as the norm.

FOOTNOTES

1. FAO (1996): *The Sixth World Food Survey*, Food and Agricultural Organisation, Rome.
2. FAO (2000): *The State of Food Insecurity in the World*, Food and Agricultural Organisation, Rome.
3. Sukhatme P V (1993): 'Note' in *Report of the expert Group on Estimation of Proportion and Number of Poor*, Perspective Planning Division, Planning Commision, Government of India.
4. Gopalan C, B V Ramasastri and S C Balasubramanian (2000): *Nutritive Value of Indian Foods*, revised and updated by B S Narasinga Rao, Y G Deosthale and K C Pant, National Institute of Nutritional, Hyderabad.